# SIGNATURES OF THE STARS

BY KEVIN MARTIN

AN INSIDER'S GUIDE TO CELEBRITY AUTOGRAPHS

# SIGNATURES OF THE STARS

BY KEVIN MARTIN

AN INSIDER'S GUIDE TO CELEBRITY AUTOGRAPHS

Antique Trader Books
A Division of Landmark Specialty Publications
Norfolk, Virginia

**Dedication:**

*I would like to dedicate this book to Christian and Stirling —*
*I hope you meet soon.*

**ISBN:** 0-930625-93-5
**Library of Congress Catalog Card Number:** 98-70851

**Editor:** Tony Lillis
**Art Director:** Chris Decker
**Designer:** Derek Leif Nealey
**Copy Editor:** Sandra Holcombe
**Editorial Assistant:** Wendy Chia-Klesch

*Printed in the United States of America*

To order additional copies of this book or a catalog, please contact:

**Antique Trader Books**
P.O. Box 1050
Dubuque, Iowa 52004
1-800-334-7165

# TABLE OF CONTENTS

# Acknowledgments

I would like to take a moment to thank all of the people who helped to research the material for this book. Literally thousands of auction and dealer catalog sales entries were used to arrive at pricing. Also helpful was the recognized authority in the field of pricing, *The Sanders Price Guide to Autographs*, by George and Helen Sanders. And, if you are interested in autographs beyond the field of entertainment, there are many other fine books that can be found in your local library, including *From the President's Pen*, by Michael Minor, which deals exclusively with presidential autographs; *Scribbles & Scoundrels*, by the deceased dean of autographs, Charles Hamilton; or *Forging History*, by Kenneth Rendell, just to name a few.

I wish to thank Allan Miller, managing editor at Landmark Specialty Books, for putting up with my impatient phone calls and letters as this book was being prepared. Thanks also go to editor Tony Lillis, designers Chris Decker and Derek Leif Nealey, copy editor Sandra Holcombe, and editorial assistant Wendy Chia-Klesch, for making the book a reality.

I also wish to thank all of the dealers whose support and encouragement has been greatly appreciated. Although this is by no means a complete list, some of the names that come immediately to mind are: John Rezinkoff, George and Helen Sanders, Jim and Pat Smith, Catherine Barnes, Max Rambod, Bill Miller, Joseph Madellena, and Cordelia and Tom Platt.

Last, but certainly not least, I wish to thank my other half—Andjelika—without whom this project would have never been completed.

Kevin Martin

# How to Use this Book

## Scarcity

There is an old addage among antique dealers that the time to buy an item is when you see it. The reason is simple. Unlike shopping for a pair of socks that will always be in stock at one store or another, an antique you see today may sell tomorrow, then not show up on the market again for weeks, months, or even years!

Likewise, there are autographs that are easy to obtain, like a Tom Cruise-signed photograph. There are autographs that are easy to find, like a Marilyn Monroe autograph, but expensive. And there are autographs that are scarcer than hens' teeth at any price.

If you thought, for example, that Tom Cruise was a rare autograph, you might move too quickly in buying one and pay too much—or worse, buy from an inexperienced dealer and end up with a secretarial signature. Likewise, there are signatures that show up so seldom on the market that you should buy them when you find them.

To help you in your collecting, each autograph is rated with a Scarcity Index that is made up of one to five stars:

★ A single star means that in most autograph dealers' catalogs or conventions, you will be tripping over that particular signature. Therefore, you should be choosy; get a good price and the best piece (picture image or content in a letter) that you can find.

★★ Two stars is still fairly easy to come by, so don't buy too soon for too much.

★★★ Three stars means that a piece is uncommon—not rare or scarce—but not available in every catalog or at auction. We estimate that a diligent search will turn up several examples of these pieces in less than 90 days.

★★★★ Four stars is a scarce item that may take up to a year to fill a hole in your collection. Here is the level you should consider buying when encountered. If unhappy down the road, you can trade up if you find a better offer for your tastes.

★★★★★ Five stars is the international rating for excellence in hotels, restaurants, and in this case, autographs. It means that the item is so rare (but not necessarily expensive) that you consider yourself lucky to have even found one. BUY IT! Five-star items may not be encountered by the same dealer for years.

The years of experience and dozens of dealers that helped rate the hundreds of selections in the pages to come will help you be better informed, and allow you to enjoy the hobby even more.

## Pricing

Pricing is the hardest part of any collectible field to pin down. It is not, after all, an exact science. But there are two important things to say on this subject. The first is exactly how I arrived at the prices used in this guide.

We took ACTUAL selling prices (pieces that actually sold, not just advertised) and auction records, and averaged them together, dropping the highest and lowest values to get an accurate idea of the range you have to pay for an item, which we then listed as one price closest to that range. Without a doubt, this is the most current and accurate guide of its kind in this field.

If a dealer tells you that these prices are not realistic on a given signature or photograph, they should have a reason why their individual piece is being offered at a higher price. For example, we used average pieces most commonly seen in the marketplace in average condition as our guide. Let's say you want to purchase a Marilyn Monroe check. You look it up in this guide and find that a typed check, signed, sells at $2200, with a handwritten check selling at $3000. Recently, a handwritten check was offered by a dealer at many times the $3000 price, but it was believed to be the LAST check, and perhaps the LAST thing she signed on the day of her death; therefore, it naturally carried a premium price. Content matters GREATLY in the field of autographs. All of the photograph prices listed here are based on eight-by-ten inch photographs, but an eleven-by-fourteen inch photograph, for instance, would sell for more.

All of the letter and document prices are based on normal content, but extraordinary content in a letter or document would be worth more. For example, we list that quite a few documents signed by actor Sean Connery have sold in the $150 range, but these were all legal documents dealing with aspects of the actor's financial affairs, real estate, taxes, etc. While fascinating and scarce, and irrefutably more authentic than a signature alone, a document that dealt with the terms of his employment in a movie would sell for more. If that movie were a James Bond movie, it would sell for even more. In real estate they say that three things matter to price "Location, Location, Location." With autographs, it's "Content, Content, Content." The purpose of this price guide, therefore, is to keep the neophyte collector from paying too much for a commonly encountered item.

## Pen and Ink

One way to authenticate an autograph is to know the different pen and ink types, and when each was introduced. For example, Bruce Lee died before the introduction of "Sharpies"in 1977, which is a type of marker. If a signed photograph in Sharpie was encountered, you would know it was a forgery.

The first regularly used pen and ink were fountain pens, first widely advertised in the 1870s. The stroke diameter varies on a fountain pen and forgers who try to use a fountain pen on an old sheet of paper for "authenticity" quickly find out that the ink bleeds into the fibers of the aged paper. As paper ages, its fibers spread. When the ink is applied, the effect is called "feathering." Once you see an example, like the one illustrated here, you will know what to avoid.

I signed my name quickly in a top quality fountain pen and ink on a page that was over 50 years old, and yet you can see what happens. The majority of forgeries encountered are of modern stars.

Ballpoint Pens were introduced in the late 1940s, but not widely used until around 1954. Additional ink colors were later introduced, including lavender, red, and green.

Porous, or felt tip, pens were introduced around 1963. Black-blue debuted in 1964, but these were fine line pens.

These pen's ink faded and "ghosted," which left a yellow halo effect around the writing after years. These concerns were addressed with the introduction around 1977 of a thicker marker called the "Sharpie."

The Sharpie dries fast and permanently, making it the choice among autograph hunters, and even for companies that commission celebrity signatures under contract.

Gold and silver metallic ink pens debuted in the early 1980s, but even after drying can be rubbed off easily. They are primarily used on dark photographs, for better contrast.

In the past ten years some paint pens with wild color assortments have started to hit the market, but they are too new to judge if they will deteriorate with age or not.

## Where to Find It

There are many places to find good quality material these days. Galleries are popping up in most major cities and are fun and educational. But they exist mainly for the person who is looking for only one or two pieces, already framed and ready to hang on their wall. Generally, this customer does not intend to collect any further. Because galleries have such high overhead, you will generally pay more for a piece here than you should. How much more depends on the gallery: It could be as little as the price to matt and frame the piece, to several times the value of the piece. I recently saw a framed picture of Gene Kelly from *Singing in the Rain* sell at a prominent gallery in New York City for $950, when any number of reputable dealers sell that same photograph at $75! How much is a frame worth?

Most collectors buy from a handful of dealers that issue catalogs and sell by mail. After a few purchases from different dealers you will select a few that you feel comfortable with, and that offer fair prices and good service. These dealers can be reached through collecting organizations such as the highly respected Universal Autograph Collectors Club (UACC), who themselves publish a magazine called the *Penn and Quill* for members.

Membership is for a modest fee, and the organization will expel members who have too many unresolved complaints from customers, or who have other questionable business practices.

Magazines can be found on the newstands that cater to the autograph market, but remember that a magazine is primarily concerned with being paid for their ads, and they do not guarantee that dealers within their pages are reputable.

You should never buy from any dealer who does not offer a Certificate of Authenticity with every piece sold. This guarantees the autographed items' authenticity for the lifetime of the piece, without restrictions of any kind.

You should never deal with anyone who refuses to use the postal system, relying only on UPS, FEDEX or other mailing options. Such unscrupulous dealers know that the U.S. Postal Service will prosecute dealers for mail fraud or forgery, for not issuing refunds, or selling something different than how it was described. It's always best to use a dealer with a street address, instead of just a post office box.

Ask any dealer good consumer questions, such as how long they have been in the business and whether they are full-time or part-time dealers? It takes years to become proficient in autograph authentication, and today, most dealers are learning that they must specialize in certain fields. There are dealers today that only deal in Civil War autographs, or entertainment, or even more specialized fields like The Beatles. Often these dealers are more reliable due to their focusing on one area, and not trying to be a jack of all trades.

Finally, learn all that you can. Most libraries have many fine books on the subject. The more you learn as a consumer, the wiser your choices will be, and the more you will enjoy one of the world's most "entertaining" hobbies.

## Terminology

There are a few standard terms that you should be familiar with as a collector of autographs, since they are used by most dealers and collectors when describing pieces for sale.

★ A "Sig" or "Cut" is a term for a "signature" alone on an index card or other piece of paper. When the term "album page" is used, it refers to the old-style autograph booklets that fans used to carry around for celebrities to sign. These books were very prevalent from the 1800s to the late 1950s, after which most people used regular stationery or index cards. The term "cut," incidentally, came into use to describe a signature only because, after the turn of the century, when autograph collecting became immensely popular, people didn't collect for material gain. Instead, they collected only for fun, so they often wrote a celebrity for an autograph, and when the celebrity replied in a letter, the collector "cut" their signature from the bottom of the letter and affixed it into their autograph keepsake album. Today, of course, we know the letter is more valuable than a signature alone.

★ "SP" in a description means "Signed Photograph." "ISP" stands for "Inscribed Signed Photograph," which means the photograph has been personalized or inscribed in some way, such as "Dear John" or "To Susan." In most cases, this lowers the value of the Signed Photograph.

★ "DS" in a description means a "Document Signed" by the celebrity. This is the rarest form to collect, but also the most fascinating and historical.

★ "LS" in a description means "Letter Signed," but not written by the signer. Such a letter is written by a secretary, but then signed by the celebrity. "TLS" in a description means "Typed Letter Signed" for an entirely typed letter that has been signed at the end by the celebrity. The most desirable form of letter collecting is described as an "ALS" or "Autographed Letter Signed," which simply means that the entire letter has been handwritten by the signer. "ANS" ("A Note Signed") denotes that it is a short letter of one paragraph or less.

★ For music lovers a "AMQS" or "MQS" means a bar of music has been drawn and identified from a song and signed by the composer—"A Musical Quote Signed."

★ "B/W" means that the photograph in question is a black and white photograph, and not in color. "Great Content" means that the letter or document has better than average remarks written in it by the celebrity.

These are the most common abbreviated terms that will help you when collecting autographs.

Happy Collecting!

# THE LEGENDS OF HOLLYWOOD

Selecting the hundreds of names to profile in this book from among the thousands of celebrities of the past and present was no easy task. The criteria used to select the names was based on two things: First, those entertainers who have left an undeniable mark on the American public, and second, autographs that regularly sell for twenty dollars and up.

Dozens of dealers were consulted along the way in an effort not to slight anyone in these selections, yet still you may find a favorite star of yours not listed. Even so, you will find many of your favorites, with information about them you may not have known, along with background surrounding each star's signing habits.

The purpose of the guide is also to give you an insider's view of what exists currently in the market. Which stars signed a lot? Which stars signed seldom, if at all? Which stars' personal bank checks, letters, or documents are commonly encountered in the collecting world, and which destroyed their personal paperwork, or otherwise kept it unattainable?

Knowledge is key in every collecting hobby, and many dealers do not want you to know, for instance, that over 900 of Marilyn Monroe's checks have been found. But by learning these things, and with the prices included here, you can build a smart collection for fun or investment without paying too much along the way.

**Abbott and Costello** (1895-1974 and 1906-1959)—Bud Abbott played the straight man in this legendary comedy team, while Lou Costello created the laughter. Off screen, though, the duo often didn't get along. From the start of their careers, their profits were split 40/60, with the larger share going to Costello. At one point, Lou Costello tried to get Universal to change the team's name to Costello and Abbott. Between Costello being a legend in his own mind, and Abbott being an alcoholic, they split the team up in 1956. Costello made one solo film in 1959, but died of a heart attack before it was released. Abbott died in 1974. As is often the case in multiple signatures, a collector must be careful to watch for not only secretarial signatures, but also whether or not one star signed both stars' names, which commonly occurred. Items signed by both are highly desirable and expensive, with signatures together on one page currently worth $550-650, and the pair on a photograph worth between $1000-1200. Separate signatures are—like their salaries—not an even 50/50 split in value. In death as in life, Costello's is worth more than Abbott's—probably because he died so many years before Abbott. Costello's signature runs $250-275, and Abbott's between $175-200. Documents and letters are scarcer.

**Scarcity Index—Abbott ★★ Costello ★★★ Both ★★★**

**Burns and Allen** (1896-1996 and 1902-1964)—The female and funny half of the George Burns and Gracie Allen comedy team known for her ditzy yet smart retorts to husband George, was in real life married to the actor. Burns always maintained that she was the brains of the team, and always showed a deep devotion to her after her sad passing in 1964. They were married in 1926 and began starring in films three years later. But it was radio that made them both stars, beginning in 1932 on their own weekly program which they brought successfully to TV in 1950. Gracie retired due to a heart condition in 1958—it eventually claimed her life. Incredibly, Burns reinvented himself long after retirement. In 1975, at the age of 79, he won an Academy Award for the old age film, *The Sunshine Boys*! He went on to star in a dozen films after that, including the succesful *Oh God* pictures. He died at 100 years of age, having never remarried after his beloved Gracie's death. George Burns did private signings for several autograph firms, as well as signing his fan mail until late in his 90s, when secretaries took over the chore and attempted to copy his signature. Be careful! While longevity and signing has kept Burns affordable, Gracie's signature is uncommon and commands much more. The best is an item signed by both, but like many famous teams, there are items on the market today that, while appearing to be signed by both, were actually signed (both names) by either Burns or Allen. Illustrated is an authentic example of their signatures together. Burns' signature alone costs $40, with signed photographs at $80. Burns' and Allen's signatures together run $200, with a jointly signed photograph at about $450.

**Scarcity Index—Burns ★ Allen ★★**
**Burns and Allen ★★★★**


**Rex Allen** (1922-    )—Famous western star who trailblazed through serials and films on his trusty steed "Koko." A western legend now, he frequently appears at western conventions to sign for fans, keeping his signed photographs reasonably priced. He often adds "& KOKO" after his signature.

**Scarcity Index—★**

**Tim Allen** (1953-    )—"Tim the Tool Man Taylor" as he is referred to on his hit TV sitcom, "Home Improvement," was a hit first in comedy clubs where his act on "Men's Men," com-plete with grunting, opened the doors to his own TV show. He has since hit home runs in writing (two best-selling comedy books) and has already had one hit movie for Disney, called *The Santa Clause.* After "Home Improvement's" first year on the air, Allen signed a limited number of Benford (the fictional tool company sponsors on the show) hammers in a wood box as presents and these currently sell for around $400. His signature is worth $25. He is a friendly signer in person, but as of yet has not answered fan mail. A signed photograph is worth $60, with signed images from Disney's *Toy Story* selling best. (He was the voice of the character "Buzz Lightyear.")
**Scarcity Index**—★★

**Don Ameche** (1908-1993)—Born Dominic Amici, Don Ameche had a long motion picture career that began in 1936 and spanned over 100 pictures. Even long past most people's retirement age he was winning accolades and Oscars, like he did in the 1985 movie *Cocoon.* He was always a friendly signer for his fans and even signed fan mail late in his career. His longevity and willingness to sign has kept his price affordable, with signatures valued at $25, and signed photographs at $50.
**Scarcity Index**—★

**Eddie "Rochester" Anderson** (1905-1977)—With his gravelly voice and large rolling, expressive eyes, this character actor/comedian was destined to make it in film, but it probably didn't hurt that he teamed up early with Jack Benny on radio and TV as his butler and comic foil. He also had a part in *Gone with the Wind*, which makes him needed to complete that cast, as thousands of collectors are doing. He alternated between signing "Eddie Anderson," "Rochester Anderson" (his character's name with Benny was "Rochester") or simply "Rochester." The most desirable form was, of course, "Eddie 'Rochester' Anderson," which he also signed. His signature is ever increasing in value and is uncommon.
**Scarcity Index—★★★**

**Julie Andrews** (1935-   )—Born Julia Elizabeth Wells, one of the finest voices to ever grace the stage and screen became Julie Andrews. Revenge is sweet sometimes in life; just ask Julie. While she made the part of "Eliza" famous on Broadway in *My Fair Lady*, when it came time to cast the movie version the studios felt that Julie was an unknown and cast Audrey Hepburn instead (Hepburn was not a singer, however, and they dubbed the voice of another singer onto the soundtrack.) The same year, Walt Disney felt that Julie WAS a major talent, and cast her to star in his film, *Mary Poppins*, opposite Dick Van Dyke. She won an Oscar for her role; Audrey Hepburn was not even nominated for hers! Married to director Blake Edwards (*Pink Panther* movies ...), she would hit big again as the lead in the musical *The Sound of Music*. In fact, most collectors desire signed photographs of her in one of these roles. She still does plays, having starred in a Broadway version of her earlier film *Victor, Victoria*. It is traditional for most performers on the Great White Way to be willing signers after a play, and Mrs. Andrews' signature is often acquired this way. Her signature sells for $25, with a signed photograph at $50. Some of her personal checks from the time of her career's beginning in 1964 have hit the market, and sell for around $65 each. Letters are scarcer.
**Scarcity Index—★**

**Roscoe "Fatty" Arbuckle** (1887-1933)—If more early films were preserved and shown on TV today, the comic genius of Roscoe "Fatty" Arbuckle would be better remembered. But sadly, he is best remembered for suffering from the first major Hollywood scandal. After going to a party in 1921 in which a girl was hurt and later died, he was accused of rape, and although he was aquitted of all charges after three intense trials, the press still went after him with the kind of vengeance that would likely have made him best friends with O.J. Simpson today; it likewise ruined his career. His wife stayed loyal to him throughout the trial, but then divorced him in 1925. A collector will find that his signature is quite scarce and that he signed his name different ways: "Roscoe Arbuckle," "Fatty Arbuckle," and the most desirable form, "Roscoe 'Fatty' Arbuckle." Any signature has value, with signed photographs even rarer. A signature will run $450 and a photograph $900 and up. After the trial, he often jokingly signed requests for autographs with the name "Will B. Goode," referring to the trial and his future behavior. These are interesting, but command less money than his real name. He is very rare in document form or handwritten letters.

**Scarcity Index—★★★★**

**Harold Arlen** (1905-1986)—Composer of such classics as "Stormy Weather" and that "Ole Black Magic," Arlen will always be remembered for composing Judy Garland's signature song "Over the Rainbow" for the 1939 classic film *The Wizard of Oz,* for which he won an Academy Award. He signed some in his old age, with the most valuable items relating to *Oz* such as a MQS ("Musical Quotes Signed") consisting of bars of music hand drawn by the composer and signed from one of their works. His signature sells for $150, with signed photographs at $250. A musical quote signed from *The Wizard of Oz* sold recently for $750.

**Scarcity Index—★★★★**

**George Arliss** (1868-1946)—Born in 1868, Arliss became a stage actor of note, then moved on to conquer films playing as a character actor mainly in historical pieces. He won one of the first Academy Awards for his performance in *Disraeli* in 1929, and is one of the keys that is tough to find for Oscar winner collectors. He died in 1946, which accounts for much of his scarcity, along with the fact that character actors—those men of 1000 faces— rarely were recognized in public and asked for autographs like the "stars" of the day. His signature sells at $100, with a signed photograph valued at around $150. Some letters have sold in the $150 range as well.

**Scarcity Index**—★★★

**Desi Arnaz** (1915-1986)—Desiderio Alberto Arnaz was already a famous Cuban/American bandleader when he met and married Lucille Ball. Together, they made television history beginning with the TV series that bore her name. He is credited with having pioneered multi-camera angles, the live audience, multiple cameras, syndication, taping shows, and much more that is such a mainstay of TV production today. Together, they ran their own Hollywood studio named Desilu—from a combination of each of their first names. Besides producing the "Lucy" shows, they also brought classic shows like "Mission Impossible" and "Star Trek" to the air. Desi wrote many letters to fans over the years of his retirement, and although still less common than hers, they are fairly inexpensive, with his signatures running $60, and photographs at $150. A typed letter sells for $150 as well.

**Scarcity Index**—★★★

**Jean Arthur** (1905-1991)—Spanning a long career and large body of work, Jean starred in silents in the 1920s and even enjoyed an Academy Award nomination in the 1940s. Her last film was in 1950, although she had a TV show in 1966. In-person signatures are uncommon because she was easily spooked by fans that approached her, even becoming hysterical at times. She rarely signed fan mail either, and spent her retirement years reclusively, even avoiding reporters. Her more memorable roles include the 1941 hit *The Devil and Mrs. Jones*, and *Only Angels Have Wings* in 1937. The scarcity makes her signatures sell at $100, with photographs at $200. A document sold recently for $150.
**Scarcity Index—★★★**

**Fred Astaire** (1899-1987)—Fred Astaire will always be remembered as the screen's greatest dancer. Besides his most famous co-star, Ginger Rogers, Astaire danced with the best—from Judy Garland and Leslie Caron, to Rita Hayworth. Astaire worked very hard in rehearsals to bring his magic to the screen. He died of pneumonia in 1987. He often signed in person for collectors, and even spent the last years of his retired life signing his fan mail. A signature costs around $50, with a signed photograph running $150. A few signed documents have hit the market in the past few years that run around $300. Some of his most memorable films include *Easter Parade* in 1948 and *Swing Time* in 1936.
**Scarcity Index—★★★**

**Mary Astor** (1905-1987)—Mary Astor had an incredible career that spanned over 100 motion pictures. Collectors will remember her (and need her) for *Maltese Falcon* collections, as well as *Meet Me in St. Louis* opposite Judy Garland. She is also an Academy Award-winning actress, making her collectible in that field as well as the others. She signed her fan mail for much of the last retired years of her life. Her signature is getting more uncommon, but is still fairly reasonable at $40, with signed photographs at $100.
**Scarcity Index—★★**

**Gene Autry** (1907-   )—Gene Autry has had an incredible career. It was comedian Will Rogers who first discovered him singing at a railroad station, and though he may have had a "lucky" break in this regard, it was pure talent that made him the legend called the "Singing Cowboy." He was the top western star from 1937 to 1942. As a singer, he sold 9 million records and wrote over 200 songs, including the Christmas classic "Here Comes Santa Claus." In the last few years he stopped signing fan mail, presumably due to age. He did sign much fan mail in years past, however. Demand has already pushed the price of a signature to $25, with photographs at $60. A few documents and typed letters have sold in the $100 range.
**Scarcity Index**—★★

**Lauren Bacall** (1924-   )—Born Betty Jo Ann Perske, "Baby" Bacall, as her husband and frequent co-star Humphrey Bogart called her, had already taken Hollywood by storm before meeting Bogie with her own sultry modeling style that the press nicknamed "The Look." She went from cover girl to starlet opposite Bogart in the classic *To Have and Have Not* in 1944, and starred opposite him again in *The Big Sleep* in 1946. (She eventually did two more films with him.) Marilyn Monroe fans collect her for her portrayal in *How to Marry a Millionaire* in 1953. She has just begun to accept acting roles again, and attends many charitable and social functions where she signs when approached. She has also sporadically answered her fan mail for years, which has kept her signature at a reasonable $25, and photographs at $50. Documents and letters have sold in the $100 range.
**Scarcity Index**—★

**Alec Baldwin** (1958-   )—Alec and his brothers, Stephen and William, are an acting dynasty today. He first became noticed as the befuddled husband opposite Geena Davis in the dark comedy *Beetlejuice*, starring Michael Keaton. He then achieved even bigger box office status as author Tom Clancy's vision of his literary character Jack Ryan in *The Hunt for Red October,* opposite Sean Connery. Later, he asked for too much money, and in subsequent films of Clancy's work, was replaced by Harrison Ford. He married actress Kim Bassinger and the two recently had a baby. He is a pleasant signer in person, with signatures selling for $25, and photographs selling at $50. In 1994, he played the legendary character the "Shadow" on the big screen, which is a collectible image as well.
Scarcity Index—★★

**Lucille Ball** (1911-1989)—So remembered for her TV series, many people forget that Ball starred in over 50 films, and was a chorus girl early in her career. In 1951, she began the groundbreaking comedy series "I Love Lucy" with her real life husband, Desi Arnaz. They became famous and wealthy doing the series—even buying the old RKO studios and forming their own Desilu studios—which produced hits like "Star Trek" and "Mission Impossible." She divorced Arnaz in 1960 and married comic Gary Morton, who produced her next TV series "The Lucy Show." In 1961, she tried her hand at Broadway in *Wildcat*, but it was critically panned and flopped. Only very early in her career did she sign her full name "Lucille Ball." Instead, she usually signed simply "Love Lucy." A "Love Lucy" signature will run around $75, with a signed photograph at $150, but a full signature is worth $200 plus, with a photograph signed in full at $400 plus. A few years ago, a small cache of approximately 50 documents were discovered that were "Minutes of Desilu Board Meetings" signed by the officers including Desi and Lucy. These are very desirable and range from $950-1200 today. An even smaller amount of her business checks (approx. 12) from one of her charitable accounts also hit the market at around $500 each. Photographs signed by both Lucy and Desi are uncommon and sell for $500.
Scarcity Index—★★

**John Barrymore** (1882-1942)—The Barrymores are an acting dynasty if there ever was one. Their stage work was said to be magnificent, but most were aging actors by the time they tried their hand at the silver screen. At least, that is most true about John's brother and sister, Lionel and Ethel. But John had the best luck on the silver screen and even won an Oscar. They all had trouble with alcohol, (John especially so). He starred in *Dr. Jekyll and Mr. Hyde* and played "Sherlock Holmes" (for which he is collected) opposite Roland Young in 1922. Late in his career, he was removed from pictures for forgetting lines and being inebriated. He died penniless in 1942. Actress Drew Barrymore continues the Barrymore tradition of acting. John's signature runs around $200, with a photograph at $500. Ethel's signature runs $125, with a photograph at $200. (She died in 1959.) Lionel, who died in 1954, runs around $100 and $175, respectively. Documents signed by any of the Barrymore clan are scarcer than photographs, and priced higher in each instance.

**Scarcity Index—Ethel ★★ Lionel ★★
John ★★★ Drew ★**

**Kim Bassinger** (1953-  )—Although she had appeared in a couple of films before, it was opposite Sean Connery in his farewell James Bond film *Never Say Never Again*, that she was noticed by the world. *Nine and a Half Weeks* further placed the actress in the limelight, starring in a film which pushed the erotic envelope. She is collected on photographs as Vickie Vale (*Batman*) and in sexy images. Photographs like these sell for $60, with her signature selling at $25. Some of her personal checks have hit the market and sell for around $80, with other documents and letters being scarcer.

**Scarcity Index—★★**

**Warner Baxter** (1892-1951)—Another key signature needed to collect Oscar winners is Warner Baxter, who was one of Hollywood's early leading men. Born in 1892, he starred first in silent films, then made the transition to talkies, which many male stars had trouble doing. He died of pneumonia in 1951, and his signature is quite scarce. A signature will cost $100, with a photograph at $175. Documents are rarer, but some handwritten letters have sold in the $150-200 range with normal content.

Scarcity Index—★★★

**Warren Beatty** (1937-   )—Beatty's big break undoubtedly came in the hit *Bonnie and Clyde*, opposite Faye Dunaway, when the press dubbed him the new James Dean. (He would certainly rise to their expectations off screen.) His next big successes were the 1975 hit *Shampoo*, which he starred in and produced, and *Heaven Can Wait*, in 1978. He won an Oscar as director for the movie *Reds* in 1981, and is remembered lately for the 1989 hit *Dick Tracy*, which starred Madonna (with whom he was having an off-screen fling). He married actress Annette Benning in 1993, and the couple has three children. He does sign in public occasionally, but not fan mail as of yet. A signature runs $30, with a photograph at $60. A few documents pertaining to his movies have sold in the $250 range. Letters are scarce. (Wouldn't you love to buy his diary?)

Scarcity Index—★★

**Wallace Beery** (1886-1949)—A character actor from the silents to the talkies, Beery won an Academy Award in 1932 for *Dr. Jekyll and Mr. Hyde* (tied with Fredric March). He is one of the keys in an Oscar collection, and is uncommon in all forms. A signature costs $125, and a photograph $250. Documents are scarce for Beery, as are handwritten letters, and would cost more than photographs. He died of a heart attack in 1949, which accounts for much of this scarcity.

Scarcity Index—★★★

**Ralph Bellamy** (1904-1991)—Although he won a Lifetime Achievement Oscar in 1986, Bellamy will probably be most remembered as the millionaire brother opposite Don Ameche in the Eddie Murphy movie *Trading Places*. He was always a willing signer in person and signed fan mail for years—keeping his signature affordable at $30, and signed photographs at $75. Letters and documents sell in the same $75 range.
**Scarcity Index—★**

**John Belushi** (1942-1982)—One of many famous comedians to emerge from the "Second City" comedy team before becoming one of the original "Not Ready For Prime Time Players" on the TV show "Saturday Night Live." He went on to have many hit films most memorably *Animal House*. Acting wasn't his only forte, which he proved by taking a comedy sketch about two Blues singers all the way to a major movie and an album that spawned a hit record, "The Blues Brothers." His high lifestyle of drugs and alcohol eventually claimed his life, and he died in a lone bungalow at the Beverly Hills Hotel in 1982. Dying so suddenly at the height of fame has pushed his signature value high, at $300, with signed photographs at $600. A small number (approx. 20) of personal checks signed by him were sold shortly after his death by his widow, Judy Jacklin. These checks currently sell for $600 each.
**Scarcity Index—★★★★**

**Jack Benny** (1894-1974)—Benny's famous stage persona as a mean-spirited tightwad was directly opposed to the way friends and colleagues remember him offscreen. His greatest fame came on radio and TV with his ever faithful sidekick "Rochester," played by Eddie Anderson. The image of his hand to chin and with a violin will be remembered for decades to come. Sadly, Benny died in 1974 just as he was about to do his first film in 30 years, *The Sunshine Boys*. George Burns would replace him and win an Academy Award for his performance, essentially re-launching his own career. Benny in retirement years would often answer mail from fans, and was a gracious signer in person. His signature runs $60, with a photograph at $150 and up. Many signed typed letters have been on the market and, depending on content, run $150 and up.
**Scarcity Index—★★**

**Ingrid Bergman** (1915-1982)—At the height of her career, Ingrid Bergman was the top box office female draw in the country. She is collected today mainly by *Casablanca* collectors for having starred opposite Bogart in the classic film, but her long career would include many roles and Oscar wins. Still tops in the public eye, she fell in love with, and had a baby out of wedlock with, Italian director Rossellini in 1950. The American public was outraged at her "immoral" actions, which poisoned her career for nearly twenty years. In the 1970s, she returned to do some good pictures, and was one of the first actresses to do films as an older woman and not trying (face lifts, etc.) to keep back the hands of time. She died of cancer in 1982, just months after finishing a critically acclaimed TV mini-series about the life of Israeli Premier Golda Meir. She was always a willing signer for fans, but was often out of the country. Therefore, supply is low while demand, due to *Casablanca* and other films, will always be high. A signature runs around $150, with a photograph at $250 and up; a photograph in character from *Casablanca* would sell for more.
**Scarcity Index—★★★**

**Clara Blandick** (1880-1962)—One of the rarest *Wizard of Oz* signatures, Blandick played Dorothy's "Aunt Em" in the classic film. She died over 45 years ago and is, therefore, very scarce. A signature sells at $350, with signed photographs (none are known in character as "Aunt Em") selling for $600. A rare document sold at auction a couple of years ago for $1200.
Scarcity Index—★★★★★

**Humphrey Bogart** (1899-1957)—Undoubtedly, no other single actor has had so many biographies written about him as "Bogie." In the 1940s, this man—who became an actor by accident, had a speech impediment, and was neither tall nor terribly handsome—would become a star and stay at the top of the box office heap for twenty years. Collectors will find that any actor or vintage Hollywood collection, or any Oscar-winner collection is incomplete without him. (He won for *The African Queen*.) His fourth wife was young starlet Lauren Bacall, with whom he would co-star several times. (Remember her line, "All you have to do is whistle.") He loved her deeply, nicknaming her "Baby," which she sometimes signed when out with "Bogie." He never signed his own famous nickname and was angered any time anyone called him by it. He was not overly friendly when it came to signing autographs, even stating once that "all an actor owed his fans was a good performance." That he gave us. His signature costs $900-1100, and a signed photograph costs $2500-3000. Some very rare items that surfaced a few years back were handwritten postcards with chess moves on them that he sent to a friend while on the set of *Casablanca*. He played an ongoing game in the mail with the friend. These few cards (approx. 12) hit the market about seven years ago, and the last reported sale of one was for $4000. Documents are very rare, and start at $2500 when encountered. His value will surely only increase "As Time Goes By."
Scarcity Index—★★★★

**Ray Bolger** (1904-1988)—Who can forget the first time they saw Bolger dance as the "Scarecrow" in the classic film *The Wizard of Oz?* An intensely friendly man, Bolger often signed for fans in person, as well as his fan mail. He attended nostalgia conventions in his later years, signing at those as well. He signed a few items under contract, most notably an *Oz* poster with co-stars Jack Haley, Margaret Hamilton, and various actors and actresses that portrayed Munchkins in the film. Even with his prodigious signing history, demand is outstripping supply, and his price continues to increase. A signature will cost $65, with a signed photograph as the Scarecrow selling for $200. Some documents and letters have sold in the same $200 range, depending on content. He even sold a dealer a small amount of straw that he had saved from his costume, which has been divided up into smaller and smaller packages and re-sold. One word of caution. He always inscribed his photographs, and the few uninscribed on the market today are the result of the owner using chemicals or other substances to remove the inscription. While the jury is still out on whether or not this practice should even occur, at least be careful to examine any uninscribed photographs for scratches or other signs that the removal was done poorly.

**Scarcity Index—★★**

**Ward Bond** (1903-1960)—From the classic John Ford western "Wagon Master" in 1950 to playing "Seth Adams," the trail cook, on the hit TV series "Wagon Train," Ward Bond is a must for any serious western collection. In fact, "Wagon Train" was the number one-rated western TV show in November 1960 when, tragically, Bond died of a heart attack. His signature is a bit scarce today, probably due to his untimely passing over 35 years ago. A signature will cost $75, with a signed western photograph at $150.

**Scarcity Index—★★★**

**Shirley Booth** (1907-1992)—This character actress seemed destined to play "Hazel," the busybody maid with a heart of gold. It earned her two Emmys for the long running TV series. She often signed fan mail prior to her death in 1992, but her signed photographs as "Hazel," as well as her signature, are getting more and more uncommon. She also is an Oscar winner for the movie *Come Back Little Sheba* in 1952, and, therefore, is collected by Oscar collectors as well as TV fans. A signature will cost $35, with a signed "Hazel" picture at $100.
**Scarcity Index—★★**

**Charles Boyer** (1897-1978)—One of only a couple of French men to make it in Hollywood (the other being Chevalier), Charles Boyer began in the silent era and easily made the transition to talkies with his dark good looks and unique accent. He died from an overdose of drugs in 1978—just days after the death of his wife—on his ranch in Arizona after a long and fruitful career. Boyer's signature is getting harder to find and has started to rise in value, currently running around $50 as a signature, and $125 on a photograph.
**Scarcity Index—★★★**

**Marlon Brando** (1924-   )—Next to Garbo, when she was alive, Brando is the most expensive signature for a living celebrity. He is notorious about not signing for fans. He employed a secretary in the 1970s to sign some mail for him, and many of these are sold as authentic by dealers who have not handled enough real Brando's to tell them apart. He is aging and overweight. (What I'm trying delicately to say is, buy one NOW if you intend to at all.) He has starred in some real classics, such as his role as Johnny in *The Wild Ones*, and the lead in *A Streetcar Named Desire*, and of course, his most collected role to date, *The Godfather*. He set tongues wagging when he came out of retirement in 1978, for the sum of $2 million, to play a five-minute cameo role as Superman's father in the first *Superman* movie starring Christopher Reeve. He is also an Oscar winner (1954 for *On the Waterfront*), but sent an American Indian to turn it down live at the awards show (he did not attend), which did not exactly go over big with the Academy. He owns his own island near Tahiti, which he lives on reclusively, although he has filmed two on-set films in Los Angeles in the last two years. While on the L.A. set, he has signed a FEW pieces—so few that it did not hurt the value of his signature, which currently runs $300 and up, and $750 plus on a  signed photograph. (*The Godfather*-signed photographs are number one in demand.) Documents are very rare, and one from the 1950s sold recently for $1500 at auction. Letters are equally scarce from this private actor, who is, nonetheless, a must for any serious collection of Hollywood stars. WATCH OUT FOR FAKES!!!
Scarcity Index—★★★★

**Charles Bronson** (1921-   )—It is hard to believe that Charles Bronson is now in his late 70s. The action star of such classics as the *Death Wish* movies is second in popularity only to Clint Eastwood in that genre. He uses a secretary to sign most of his fan mail, and the differences in the secretarial signature are obvious when compared to his authentic signature, especially in the way he signs the "B" in Bronson. Bank checks of his have hit the market and sell for $60 as do signed photographs, with a signature alone selling for $25.
Scarcity Index—★★

**Pierce Brosnan** (1952-   )—Making his first mark as a detective on the hit TV series "Remington Steele," Brosnan eventually would be cast to play the famed James Bond in the 007 flick *Golden Eye*, which was such a hit it, in turn, guaranteed Brosnan a three-picture deal as the secret agent. He did a soft comedy turn next, opposite Robin Williams in *Mrs. Doubtfire,* and was back in the action recently in the volcano disaster film *Dante's Peak.* He is a very friendly signer in person, although his fan mail is signed by secretaries. He has often even added "007" after his name for fans. His signature is currently valued at $25, with Bond photographs (the only collected image) selling at $60.

**Scarcity Index—★★**

**Billie Burke** (1885-1970)—Early in Burke's career, she was an admired and versatile actress of the stage on both sides of the Atlantic. But, by the time movies beckoned, she played, as she called it, "a bird-witted lady," so often and so deliciously that she was typecast in those roles to the hilarity of any audience who has seen the scores of films she appeared in. She married (prior to her film career) famed showgirl/cabaret director Florenz Ziegfield, and led the life of a social butterfly—which is a good thing for *Wizard of Oz* collectors, who need her signature for their collections. She played Glinda The Good Witch in the classic film. She retired from films in 1960 and died in 1970. Most signatures that trade hands are vintage from 1918-1950. A signature will cost $150, and a photograph approximately the same, because more collectors look for a signature for *Oz* collections knowing that signed photographs of Glinda are exceedingly rare. A portrait is worth roughly the same as a signature (but is harder to sell), whereas the last signed photograph of her in her *Oz* role sold for $1500. A small cache of postcard sized photographs signed in the teens and twenties have hit the market and sell for $150 each.

**Scarcity Index—★★★**

**Richard Burton** (1925-1985)—Next to Laurence Olivier, Burton is considered by many to be one of the best Shakespearean actors in films. In fact, Olivier once said to Burton (who married and divorced Liz Taylor twice), "Make up your mind. You can be a household word or a great actor." His two biggest hits would come in movies that co-starred Taylor: *Cleopatra* and *Who's Afraid of Virginia Woolf?* Late in his career his excessive drinking affected his performances and his health, eventually killing him in 1985. He lived in Europe much of his career and rarely signed fan mail. His signature is scarce, and currently sells for $100, with photographs at $250. A few documents and letters have sold in the $250 range as well.
**Scarcity Index—★★★**

**Red Buttons** (1919-  )—Born Aaron Chwatt in 1919, Red Buttons may be known for comedy, but his first role, which won him an Oscar, was for drama in 1957's *Sayonara*. He will always be collected for being an Oscar winner, with his signature selling at $20, and photographs at $40. A friendly signer in person, he has also signed fan mail.
**Scarcity Index—★**

**Nicolas Cage** (1964-  )—Nicolas Cage changed his name not so much to become a star, but to escape the star status already associated with it. Born Nicolas Coppala (nephew to the famed director), Cage wanted to make it on his own talents, not those of his famous uncle, so he changed his name. His film debut came in *Fast Times at Ridgmont High* in 1982, but his role as the good-hearted thief in *Raising Arizona*, followed by a part in *Moonstruck* opposite Cher, caused the critics to notice him. *Honeymoon in Vegas* was a hit, as was *Guarding Tess*, and he won a Golden Globe award and his first Oscar nomination for *Leaving Las Vegas*, in which he played an alcoholic, opposite Elizabeth Shue. He is a friendly signer in person, with his signature selling at $25, and signed photographs at $50. A few early documents have surfaced selling at $100 plus each.
**Scarcity Index—★★**

**James Cagney** (1899-1986)—He started his career among much praise, being considered a great dancer, singer, and versatile actor, but after a few turns playing a gangster, the public found their favorite Cagney persona. He played gangster roles so convincingly you might have thought he was one! He won an Oscar for portraying the life of George M. Cohen in the 1942 classic *Yankee Doodle Dandy*, which was definitely not gangster fare, and which should have reminded audiences of his versatility. After he retired, he refused the role of "Professor Higgins" in *My Fair Lady*, for which he was offered $1 million, and from which Rex Harrison would win an Oscar. He even turned down Harry and Tonto, which was written for him, and which would also win an Oscar for his stand-in—Art Carney. Cagney was not an eager signer for his fans, although he would sign some fan mail in his retirement years, most often signing an abbreviated "J.Cagney" instead of James or Jimmy. A full signature is worth about $100, with a "J. Cagney" worth $75. A signed photograph runs around $125 (portraits) and $200-plus in one of his many gangster roles, often brandishing a pistol. Letters (typed) have surfaced with normal content at around $150, as have a few documents in the $200 range.

**Scarcity Index—★★**

**John Candy** (1950-1994)—Friends of Candy warned him constantly of his chain smoking and love for gourmet foods. He was an accomplished cook, but it still shocked and saddened the world when we lost him to a heart attack while filming a movie in the Arizona desert. Like so many young comedians, he blazed a trail through the famed "Second City" outfit to appearing on "Saturday Night Live" and eventually headlining in his own hilarious films, such as the classic *Planes, Trains and Automobiles*, opposite Steve Martin. He was a friendly man with his fans, signing fan mail when he could, as well as signing in person. A signature sells at $50, and signed photographs at $125. A document recently sold for $150.

**Scarcity Index—★★★**

**Eddie Cantor** (1892-1964)—From the early days of burlesque to the silver screen, Cantor was one of that handful of legendary vaudeville artists who is still fondly remembered today. In 1934, he was the highest paid actor in pictures ($270,000). He retired in 1952—because of a heart attack—while still quite active in his career, and was given a special Lifetime Achievement Oscar in 1956. Cantor was affable off screen, outgoing onscreen, and appreciative of fans who asked politely for his autograph. He is found in abundance in collections from the period of his greatest fame (1920-1940s). His signature sells for about $80, with a signed photograph selling at $200. The most desirable signed photographs are of him in "blackface" and while politically incorrect today, it was an important part of his early act as it was for "Amos 'n Andy," Al Jolson, and many others. These photographs are worth $300 and up.
Scarcity Index—★★

**Jim Carrey** (1962-    )—The rubber-faced comedian from the TV series "In Living Color" is now one of the highest-paid actors in Hollywood, earning over $20 million per picture. His more memorable films include *The Mask*, and *Ace Ventura: Pet Detective*. He is starting to loosen up and become friendlier when approached to sign in person, but due to high volume, no doubt, his fan mail is answered with a pre-printed photograph. His signature sells for $35, with signed photographs selling at $75 plus, with the most collectible image currently being him as the famous villain "The Riddler" in the last Batman movie *Batman Forever*.
Scarcity Index—★★

**Lon Chaney, Sr.** (1883-1930)—What the Barrymores were to the Broadway stage and silver screen, the father and son Chaneys were to famous horror films. Lon Chaney, Sr., thrilled audiences as the "Man of 1,000 Faces," which was not only a nod at his prowess as an accomplished character actor, but also because he often undertook roles which involved complete transformations of himself by makeup—which he expertly applied himself! He first starred on the stage as a youngster (because his brother owned a theater), then in dozens of short films—as the villain in westerns mostly—but came to worldwide attention playing a contortionist in *The Miracle Man* in 1919. He would star steadily in films over the next few years, but struck it big when Universal cast him to play "Quasimodo" in *The Hunchback of Notre Dame*. He won such rave reviews (and the film made so much money) that Universal cast him in another Paris horror story, *The Phantom of the Opera* in 1925, which was another Chaney classic. In 1928, he played the screen's first vampire in *London After Midnight*, to rave reviews again. Because of this film's success, he was cast in Universal's epic *Dracula*, but he was diagnosed with fatal throat cancer while doing the film before Bela Lugosi stepped into the role. Chaney's son, who was just starting in pictures, changed his name in tribute to his father from Creighton Chaney to Lon Chaney, Jr., (1907-1973) in 1930, the year of his father's death. Chaney Jr. would not receive any of his father's accolades as a serious actor, but would become a major presence in the horror genre, most notably as the "Wolfman" in the film by the same name. Chaney Sr. was so much a character actor with makeup, etc., that he was virtually unrecognized outside of studio functions. Coupled with his dying so young over 66 years ago, his signature is very rare. When encountered, it is often in pencil, which was more in use in the teens and twenties by fans seeking autographs. His signature sells for $1200. He rarely signed photographs or answered mail, preferring to bestow signed photographs on friends in the business with him, and then of roles he himself enjoyed playing, which were often not the horror roles. A portrait or lesser known role on an 8" x 10" will fetch $1500 and up, with a "Hunchback" photo bringing $2500 and up. Chaney Jr. would occasionally sign in person as well as fan mail, but is getting scarce himself. He died in 1973. A signature of Jr. is worth $350, with a portrait signed photograph around $500. However, a monster role such as the "Wolfman" or "Frankenstein" on an 8" x 10" will bring $1000 easily. Signed letters of Chaney Jr. or Sr. are seldom encountered. An early document of Chaney Jr. recently sold for $1000, while a Sr. document was offerred recently at $4000.
**Scarcity Index—Chaney Sr. ★★★★★  Chaney Jr. ★★★**

**Charlie Chaplin** (1889-1977)—There is perhaps no other artist who has inspired such critiques and adulation. His "Little Tramp" character, and the actor who played him, will be remembered as genius in the field of comedy—on this most everyone can agree. His character ran the gamut of emotion from pathos to hilarity, with what seemed for the actor to be the most natural ease in the world. In real life he had a great ego, perhaps rightly so, and was never an easy signature to get. In fact, his vintage signed material is the most valuable, since those pieces he signed in his late seventies—after a resurgence in popularity—were signed with smaller, shakier, and usually abbreviated signatures (such as "C. Chaplain" or "Chas. Chaplain" instead of a full "Charles" or "Charlie.") Because forgers love to forge shaky signatures, his pieces signed later in life are worth less on the market than vintage pieces. Size of photographs, and whether or not he is the tramp character in those photographs, affect the price as well. A vintage signature is $350-400, with a photograph that is smaller than an 8" x 10" selling for around $550 (a portrait) and $800 as the "Tramp." An 8" x 10" vintage photograph, signed, depicting him as the "Tramp" is worth $1300 easily, with an 8" x 10" portrait worth around $900. Letters and documents are rarely encountered. A signed one-page document sold recently for $1000. He also, on rare occasion, would draw a small sketch of his famous shoes, hat, and cane, signed at the finish. These are very nicely executed and command high prices today of $1500 plus.

Scarcity Index—★★★★

**Cher** (1946-  )—Famous for her off screen personality and relationships—including her marriage and divorce to Sonny Bono—Cher, born Cherilyn Sarkesan, has proven to be a great actress in addition to singer, even winning an Oscar for her performance in the film *Moonstruck*. She is a tough signer, however, and sells for $35 as a signature and $75 plus on a photograph. She signed the most during her outings on Broadway, in plays such as *Come Back to the 5 and Dime Jimmy Dean*.

Scarcity Index—★★★

**Maurice Chevalier** (1888-1972)—Debonair, with cane and straw hat, Maurice Chevalier's unique accent made every song he sang, such as "Thank Heaven for Little Girls," from *GIGI* unforgettable. His accent was, sad to say, a fake! He was contractually required to maintain his "accent" in interviews and any time he appeared outside of the studio's protective gates. He appeared in a classic "I Love Lucy" episode once as himself, singing with Desi Arnaz. When health kept him from working in later years, he became a recluse, passing away on New Year's Day in 1972. Because of this behavior, most signatures are from his heyday, when he was a vivacious personality and willing signer for his fans. A signature is worth $60, with a signed photograph selling for $150.
**Scarcity Index—★★**

**Julie Christie** (1941-   )—Collected by Oscar collectors for her Best Actress win in 1965 for *Darling*, and as "Lara" in the film classic *Dr. Zhivago*. Christie has always been a reclusive signer, keeping her signature scarce. Maybe this is the result of all of the public attention over her long affair with equally reclusive Warren Beatty, whom she also appeared opposite in *Shampoo* and *Heaven Can Wait*. Her signature sells at $35, with signed photographs at $75.
**Scarcity Index—★★★**

**Claudette Colbert** (1903-1994)—Claudette could play comedy or dramatic roles with equal ease. Comedy was her forte, and one of her most classic films, *It Happened One Night*, opposite Clark Gable, showed her talents off nicely. After retiring and not being before the cameras in over thirty years, Colbert appeared as the wealthy matriarch in the TV movie *The Two Mrs. Greenvilles* in 1987, and looked as youthful as ever. Afterwards, she retired to her home in Barbados, where she passed away. In the seventies and eighties she sometimes answered fan mail from her home in Barbados, but had slowed the last few years (perhaps due to age). There is no shortage of her signature at $25, or $100 on a photograph. A document, which is less common, sold for $150 recently. Letters are uncommon as well.
**Scarcity Index—★**

**Ronald Colman** (1891-1958)—From 1927 to 1932, Ronald Colman was voted the top male star in the country. He was a sex symbol for nearly thirty years and was one of the few major male stars who easily made the transition from silent films to the talkies. He died in 1958, of pneumonia, while still active as an actor. He was a willing signer if approached in person, although like most superstars of the golden age of Hollywood, he employed secretaries to sign his fan mail. A signature costs $60, with a photograph at $150. A few letters have been available in the same $150 range. Documents are scarcer.
**Scarcity Index—★★**

**Sean Connery** (1930-   ) —Sean Connery is a brilliant actor who managed to break from the James Bond typecasting to win Oscars and expand as an actor with each new carefully picked role. Born in 1930, he is still actively working (three films in 1997) but is one of the toughest of all the signers. When he does sign in person, it will rarely be more than one piece, and he lives in Scotland, making it hard to get him to sign at all. Occasionally, fan mail comes signed out of Scotland, but it is his brother signing it for him. While similar, there are differences between the two. One quick way to tell is the "Best Wishes" that accompanies each of his brother's signatures. In person, he never inscribes, and surely wouldn't write, "Best Wishes." His signature is quite popular and valuable, and for the above reasons, scarce. A very few (approx. 25) checks were found and sold in the $200 range. A few other documents have sold in that range, as well. His signature is worth $75 easily, with a photograph of him as Bond (the most collectible image) selling for $250.
**Scarcity Index—★★★**

**Gary Cooper** (1901-1961)—One of the most successful stars of the Golden Age of Hollywood, Cooper, or "Coop" as his friends often called him, starred at the top of the box office for nearly thirty-five years. He won two Oscars (*Sgt. York* and *High Noon*) and, therefore, is sought by Academy Award collectors. But he is also a necessary addition to any serious collection of the Golden Age of Hollywood. Sports fans collect him because of his performance as Lou Gehrig in the 1942 movie *The Pride of the Yankees*. A month before he died of cancer in 1961, he won another Oscar, for Lifetime Achievement. His signature will cost $250-300 today, and a photograph $600-750. A few letters have surfaced in the $400-500 range, and many documents have hit the market in the last few years ranging in price from $400-750, except for full motion picture contracts. Two years ago, a full motion picture contract for his Academy Award-winning *High Noon* sold at auction for $3500, and a full motion picture contract for *The Hanging Tree* sold for $1600 a few months later.
**Scarcity Index—★★★**

**Kevin Costner** (1955-   )—Costner's career today is as a big box office star, but he started as a corpse! He is shown as a corpse several times in the classic film *The Big Chill*, not exactly a stretch for an actor, admittedly. But by the time of *The Untouchables* in 1987, he would be noticed standing up! The baseball film *Bull Durham* was a hit for him, as was *Field of Dreams*. He made his directing debut with *Dances with Wolves*, and won an Oscar as Best Director for it! Other classic images collected on photographs of Costner are from *Robin Hood, Wyatt Earp,* and *JFK*. He is a hesitant signer and uses secretaries to sign his mail. (They often write "See You at the Movies") Therefore, an authentic Costner brings $35, with $75 common on photographs.
**Scarcity Index—★★★**

**Broderick Crawford** (1911-1986)—Specializing in bad guy villains and dark characterizations, Crawford nabbed an Oscar for *All the Kings Men*, making him forever collectible to anyone who wants to build a complete set of Oscar winners. By and large, the rest of his career is full of good solid performances, but nothing too distinguished. He died in 1986 after suffering a series of strokes over several years. He signed some fan mail in his later years, and today his signature can be bought for $35, with signed photographs at $100. A document sold last year for $150, as did a letter with normal content in it.
**Scarcity Index—★★**

**Joan Crawford** (1906-1977)—Born Lucille LeSeur, Joan Crawford was the consummate movie star, refusing to let even personal acquaintances see her without makeup. She is probably remembered now as much for her "strict" upbringing of her children (including hitting them with wooden coathangers) as she is as an actress. As an actress, she is best remembered for a professional lifelong feud with fellow thespian Bette Davis, her co-star in the classic *Whatever Happened to Baby Jane*. She married Alfred Steele, who was CEO of Pepsi Cola, and took over his business duties on the Board of Directors when he died. She was a "tough broad" to be sure, but with an obvious neediness and compassion for her fans. She was corresponding by mail with over 1500 fans at the time of her death. These typed letters on her familiar blue stationery are beginning to dry up and increase in value. She was always willing to sign in person throughout her career, as well, and coupled with her extraordinary signing habits once retired, her signature currently sells for $60. A letter with normal content, signed in full, is worth $200, but MOST of those letters are signed only "Joan," and are worth roughly half of the value of a letter signed in full. Handwritten letters and documents are scarcer.
**Scarcity Index—★★**

**Bing Crosby** (1905-1977)—If you had to name the most popular entertainer of all time, Crosby might take the title. Consider these statistics: from 1930—and for over 20 years—he sold more records than any other artist, and for ten consecutive years, he was voted number one male star at the box office, and set record film grosses that stood for twenty years. He even had the top show on radio for over 15 years. He will always be remembered for singing "White Christmas," which sold more records than any other song to this day (he debuted it in the film *Holiday Inn*) and for the wildly successful "Road" pictures he made with Bob Hope and Dorothy Lamour. He died in 1977 at the age of 76. His signature is worth $60, with signed photographs at $175. Numerous letters that have hit the market over the years stay around the $100 mark because they were usually signed just "Bing," although a letter signed in full would be worth more. By the way, here's an inside tip: He often signed documents "Harry Crosby," his real name.
Scarcity Index—★★

**Tom Cruise** (1962-  )—Like so many stars, there was a time when this young hot actor would sign for fans everytime he encountered one. But today, it is tough to get him to sign, and now that he has adopted two children, he is even more reclusive in a desire to shield them from the press. His signature currently sells for $50, with a signed photograph selling at $100. Documents that have hit the market sell in the $400 range. Like many stars that have signed a lot in public, Cruise's signature years ago was legible down to each letter, but currently is more abbreviated, as shown in our examples. We have illustrated a vintage signature from the start of his career (1983), and one signed this past year to compare. He was born on July 3, 1962, as Thomas Cruise Mapother IV.
Scarcity Index—★★★

**Tim Curry** (1946-    )—If he had never made another movie after his first, Curry would forever be collected as "Dr. Frank N' Furter" from *The Rocky Horror Picture Show*, a cult movie that has played at midnight theaters for over 20 years. It is as "Frank N' Furter" that he is most collected on signed photographs, selling for $50, with signatures at $25. He is a friendly signer in person, but has not as of yet signed any fan mail. Other memorable roles include *Legends, It, Clue, Home Alone II, The Hunt for Red October,* and *Oscar.*

**Scarcity Index**—★★

**Jamie Lee Curtis** (1958-    )—Most people who star in a bunch of B horror flicks wouldn't have advanced to major female leading lady, but that's exactly what Curtis has done. She has gone from films like *Halloween*, as a scream queen, to playing opposite John Travolta in *Perfect* and Arnold Schwarzenegger in *True Lies*. She is a fairly tough signer in person, however, and is scarce on photographs in *authentic* material. The problem is many dealers have been selling the secretarial signatures they get back in the mail for years. The ironic thing about this mistake is that a bonafide legendary actress *is* signing her mail: her mother, Janet Leigh of *Psycho* fame. But, Jamie Lee is *not* signing it, and she has a very distinctive signature that looks nothing like her mother's neat cursive signature. An authentic Jamie Lee Curtis photograph sells for $75 plus, with a signature at $30. A few documents have sold in the $150 plus range. Most sexy photographs are collectible, which include images from films like *Perfect, Trading Places, A Fish Called Wanda,* and *True Lies.*

**Scarcity Index**—★★★

**Tony Curtis** (1925-   )—Like so many men with the name Tony, it is short for Anthony, and he actually signed early photographs in his career as Anthony Curtis. These photographs fetch a bit more than regular ones, bringing around $150 versus $60 for the ones signed later in life. His signature sells for $20, which is reasonable due to his own generous signing habits by mail and in person, especially over the last few years. He will always be collected for the Marilyn Monroe classic *Some Like it Hot*, and he turned in a great comedic performance opposite Cary Grant in *Operation Petticoat*. He married and divorced actress Janet Leigh, and had a daughter with her, actress Jamie Lee Curtis.
Scarcity Index—★

**Timothy Dalton** (1946-   )—Any actor who plays the famous spy, James Bond, will always be collected. Dalton played the super spy twice, and it is as Bond that he is collected on photographs at $50, with his signature alone selling at $25. He is a friendly signer in person, but has signed, infrequently, his fan mail.
Scarcity Index—★★

**Jane Darwell**  (1879-1967)—Although starring in such bit parts as housekeepers and nannies opposite young Shirley Temple early in her career, actress Jane Darwell hit her acting stride later when she landed the role of "Ma Joad" in the classic *The Grapes of Wrath,*  for which she also won an Oscar. She is collected by Disney fans for portraying the "Bird Woman" in *Mary Poppins,* and by *Gone With the Wind* collectors for appearing in that film. Being a great character actress makes one hard to recognize on the street, and very few signatures from fans' album books that appear on the market include her signature. She died after the *Mary Poppins* release in 1967. She is a scarce autograph today, valued at $100 plus, with signed photographs selling at $200. A document sold this past year at auction for $250.
Scarcity Index—★★★★

**Marion Davies** (1897-1961)—Famous throughout the silent era as a leading lady, she stopped starring in movies by the time talkies emerged. She had her own personal fortune as well as her lover: famous newspaperman William Randolph Hearst. He died in 1951 and she died in 1961. She was always a friendly signer in person, but is still a scarce signature, having been deceased for over 35 years. A signature will run around $50, with a signed photograph reaching $150.

**Scarcity Index—★★★**

**Bette Davis** (1908-1989)—Intense and electrifying in every part she played, whether as an actress or royalty, Bette Davis shaped her career by selecting her own parts and playing them to the hilt! She always felt ugly and unglamorous, and perhaps her intense and ferocious acting was to compensate for that, which it certainly did! She excelled playing "bitchy" roles, which she began with the film *Cabin in the Sky* in 1932, and which would be a theme for the rest of her career. Her greatest reviews come from, and the golden age of her career began with, *Jezebel* in 1938, for which she won an Oscar. Many fans loved her films opposite Erol Flynn, and the classic *Whatever Happened to Baby Jane*, opposite rival Joan Crawford. She signed often when fans approached her, and in retirement years often answered her mail. She died in 1989. Signatures run $50, with photographs in the $200 range. Letters usually sell for $150 plus.

**Scarcity Index—★★**

**Sammy Davis Jr.** (1925-1990)—An actor, singer, and dancer, Sammy Davis was what Hollywood directors called the "Triple Threat" type of performer. He spun number one hits in music, such as the "Candy Man," and starred opposite Dean Martin, Frank Sinatra, and other members of the infamous "Rat Pack" for years before succumbing to cancer in 1990. He rarely had time to sign fan mail, but was a very friendly signer in person, often signing backstage at his sold-out one-man shows in Las Vegas. A signature will cost $40, with signed photographs at $100. A few documents and checks have sold in the $100-plus range, as well.

**Scarcity Index—★★**

**Doris Day** (1922-   )—Born in 1922 as Doris Kappelhoff, Doris Day took the girl-next-door image to career heights. Watching the sweetness pour off the screen in one of Doris Day's performances, you would expect that she would go out of her way to sign for fans. And she has done just that for years. Although a document relating to one of her famous Rock Hudson films (*Pillow Talk*) sold at auction for $300, her signatures sell for $20, with signed photographs in the $40 range.
**Scarcity Index—★**

**James Dean** (1931-1955)—Along with Marilyn Monroe, Dean sits on top of the entertainment heap in terms of scarcity and price. Many stars have died young and tragically, but none that have developed such a worldwide following as Dean. He only completed a few films, and his most famous film was released after his death in a car crash in 1955. *Rebel Without A Cause* will always be collected, but is very tough to find. His signature sells easily in the $1500-2000 range, with photographs selling for $4500 and up. A very few of his personal checks have sold for $4000, and some other documents (non-checks) have sold for $7500 and up. Letters are very rare. Dean was an amateur artist who had obvious talent and often did oil paintings, which were given away to friends and family. One such painting sold last year for $12,000. A few signatures on grade school papers sold at auction a few years ago for around $800 per signed homework page. They were signed in grade school as "Jimmy" Dean.
**Scarcity Index—★★★★**

**Olivia DeHavilland** (1916-   )—Born in 1916, this great actress has a large body of work, but Olivia DeHavilland will still be most remembered for playing "Melanie" opposite Vivien Leigh in the classic *Gone with the Wind*, in 1939. Selznik actually wanted Joan Fontaine (Olivia's sister) to play Melanie, but when he decided in screen tests that she wasn't right for the part, it was Joan who suggested he try her sister, Olivia. She won two Oscars later in her career, and has always been gracious to fans asking for her signature (as any Southern Belle would)! She signed fan mail from her home in Paris, France, until just a couple of years ago, when she sent out letters stating she was working on her autobiography. Only last year she signed 400 8" x 10" photographs for a sports autograph dealer. She has since said that she had an unpleasant experience with. What a shame for a great lady who has always tried to please her fans. These photographs are currently being marketed for $50 each which is a bargain for such a talent as her, and one of only six surviving *GWTW* cast members. Handwritten letters are scarcer and run $200 plus, depending on content. A signature alone is $30, and documents are uncommon, selling for around $150.
**Scarcity Index—★★**

**Catherine Deneuve** (1943-   )—A beautiful blond French actress of such films as Indochine and The Last Metro, Deneuve has always been a tough signer in person and by mail. Her signature is uncommon, selling at $25, with signed photographs at $75.
**Scarcity Index—★★★**

**Bo Derek** (1956-   )—Director John Derek has always had good taste in younger wives, marrying actress Ursula Andress, then Linda Evans, and lastly, Bo Derek, who blasted into much of the male population's conscious in the movie *10*, starring Dudley Moore. She appeared nude in most of her films (she was not cast as an acting giant, after all) and is a fairly scarce autograph, living out of the country and starring in few films since *10*. Her signature sells for $30, with her photographs (*10* is most collected) selling for $75 plus.
**Scarcity Index—★★★**

**Andy Devine** (1905-1977)—Devine had a weight problem throughout his career and a distinctive scratchy voice, but these qualities were to work for him rather than against him (as the stage driver, for example, in the classic *Stagecoach*, which assured his future fame). He played sidekick to Roy Rogers in a series of films and Guy Madison's TV sidekick on the "Wild Bill Hickok" show. Other memorable western roles include *The Man Who Shot Liberty Valance* and *The Way the West Was Won*. He was a very friendly signer in person and signed a small amount of fan mail before his death. A signature runs $40—with a good western image, signed photograph selling at $100.
Scarcity Index—★★★

**Marlene Dietrich** (1904-1992)—Every bit as much as Garbo, Dietrich did it her own way. She almost single-handedly promoted feminism in her manly displays of sensuality on screen. German in descent, Hitler ordered her to return to Germany during WWII, and in typical Dietrich fashion, she refused. He banned her films. She said she liked playing the "sleazy girl all the men had to fight over," but American audiences were not so endeared to her performances despite great critical reviews. Long after retiring from films, she made her New York stage debut in 1967, but left that when the crowds dwindled. In 1984, she was interviewed for a biographical TV special that she herself produced called "Marlene," although by then she refused to be photographed. She signed fan mail often the last few years of her retired life and literally hundreds of photographs were signed by her in these years. Thus, the price has been reasonable for a long time, but the supply is drying up, with her signed photographs running $200 and signatures at $65. Letters are scarce, but a few documents have surfaced selling in the $200 range.
Scarcity Index—★★

**Divine** (1945-1988)—The most famous 300-pound female impersonator in the world. O.K, maybe the only one. Divine was kept busy starring in films by director and close personal friend John Waters. Most of his/her appearances are cult favorites today with the only real commercial success coming in 1988 for the campy film *Hairspray*. Tragically, he died 10 days after the film's release. His signature is scarce and sells for $100 today, with signed photographs selling at $200.
**Scarcity Index—★★★**

**Kirk Douglas** (1916-    )—Recently during the annual Oscars show, a courageous Douglas took the stage to accept a Lifetime Achievement Award, sweetly thanking his sons in the audience, actors Michael and Eric Douglas. It was obvious to all of his fans that Kirk had suffered a stroke. It seems that he has retired now for good and his shaking even stopped his rather generous past habits of signing fan mail. He is still fairly easy to find, but there is nowhere to go but up for the price of this legendary actor of so many films. His most collected photographic image seems to be as "Spartacus," which sells currently for $65 (cheap!), with his signature at $25. In the last several years, he has had modest success as a writer of fiction, publishing three books to date.
**Scarcity Index—★**

**Marie Dressler** (1869-1934)—Depression-era audiences loved Dressler for much the same reasons the studios thought she would fail—because she was heavy, unattractive, and played realistic characters like drunks and women whose husbands cheated on them. She was a great actress and fine comedian and was recognized with one of the first Academy Awards, which makes her a necessary addition to an Oscar collection. She died in 1934 of cancer, however, and is, therefore, a scarce signature to obtain. A signature will cost $150 plus, with a photograph at 250 plus. Letters are uncommon and sell in the $250 range, as do documents.
**Scarcity Index—★★★★**

**Clint Eastwood** (1930-   )—It was one of my articles published in an autograph magazine that uncovered that Clint Eastwood has used the same secretary to sign his fan mail for more than 10 years. The article sent dealers running for cover and refunding prior pieces they had sold. I first researched it because it had all seemed too good to be true (and it was) that a man could sign a large volume of fan mail while starring in one film, directing another, and being mayor of a California town. His authentic signature is similar to the one in the mail, but there are distinct differences in them. Be careful not to buy a secretarial signature of him; the quickest indicator of one is that the small "d" at the end of Eastwood looks like a small "g," with no upward sweep to it (only downward), as opposed to his real signature that is clearly a "d." A few documents have sold in the $200 range, as have letters. Like many modern stars, his signature has gotten more abbreviated as the years have gone by, with some in the 1970s being quite legible and full. However, it now reads more like "Cl Eastwood." His signature is worth $35, with western-signed photographs (the most collectible images) at $100 plus. He won an Oscar for the movie *Unforgiven*, which he directed and starred in, giving further reason to collect this legendary star (as if we needed another one)!
**Scarcity Index—★★**

**Buddy Ebsen** (1908-   )—If he had not developed a severe allergic reaction to the ground aluminum in the makeup, Ebsen would have been the "Tin Man" in *The Wizard of Oz* instead of Jack Haley. (In fact, he had already started filming.) But he went on to star, instead, opposite Shirley Temple and other legends as a good supporting actor before finding his fame on TV with the long running series "Beverly Hillbillies" and later "Barnaby Jones." It is as "Jed Clampett" that he is most collectible on photographs, selling at $50, with a signature at $20. Documents have sold in the $75 range as have letters. He has always been a friendly signer in person and spent much of the last ten years answering fan mail, although stopping in recent years probably due to age.
**Scarcity Index—★★**

**Leon Errol** (1881-1951)—A popular character actor opposite Lupe Valez in her *Mexican Spitfire* films, as well as *Joe Palooka* films, and over 100 other comedies. Errol also starred in the *Invisible Man's Revenge* and the W.C. Fields classic *Never Give a Sucker an Even Break*. A scarce signature sells for $50, with signed photographs at $100 plus. **Scarcity Index—★★★**

**Douglas Fairbanks, Sr.** (1883-1939)—Douglas Sr. was born Douglas Ulman in 1883. He first hit the stage in 1903, but jumped eagerly into films just as they were coming into their own in 1915. His boyish smile and athletic prowess were put to good use in film after film. In the 1920 classic, *The Mark of Zorro*, Fairbanks had at last found his ideal starring vehicle. *Robin Hood*, *Son of Zorro*, *Thief of Bagdad*, and *The Black Pirate* all followed. He married one of the most famous female stars at the time, America's sweetheart, Mary Pickford. Fairbanks and wife Pickford, along with their friend Charlie Chaplin and D.W. Griffith, formed their own studio to give more control to the stars, and called it United Artists, producing and distributing their own pictures. In 1936, he retired from pictures and died in his sleep of a heart attack in December 1939. Son **Douglas Fairbanks, Jr.,** (1909- ) never did achieve the kind of stardom of his famous father, perhaps because his dad cast such a long shadow from which to escape. He has had a long and prolific career, however. He will sign fan mail often, and make appearances on the convention circuit, where he signs photographs from his movies. The abundance of Jr.'s signature has kept his price at $15, with photographs running $30, but his famous father is another story. He died in 1939 and spent much of those last years in Europe. Only vintage signatures obtained in person exist and will cost $200 plus, with photographs at $350 plus. Documents and letters of Fairbanks Sr. are scarce, but exist much more commonly on Fairbanks Jr., and in sufficient quantities to currently satisfy collector demand.

**Scarcity Index— Fairbanks Sr. ★★★★ Fairbanks Jr. ★**

**Jose Ferrer** (1912-1992)—A stage and screen star, his greatest successes came on the stage, although he is an Oscar winner and is collected for this reason. He also starred in such classic films such as *Joan of Arc*, and his breakout role in *Cyrano DeBergerac*, for which he won the Oscar. His last film was in 1989. Today, he rarely answers fan mail, although he does sign in person when approached. His signature sells for $25, with a photograph at $60. A few letters have sold in the $100 range, and he sometimes signed letters with a caricature of himself as Cyrano instead of a signature.
**Scarcity Index—★★**

**W.C. Fields** (1879-1946)—No comedy collection could be considered complete without a W.C. Fields signature in it. In movies, he drank to excess, lied, and was a loser—and the public loved him! Offscreen, he was a lot like his onscreen persona! His most famous films came late in his career. *The Bank Dick*, *My Little Chickadee*, *You Can't Cheat an Honest Man*, and *Never Give a Sucker an Even Break*. He died on Christmas Day in 1946. He was a tough signature to obtain in person and never answered fan mail. Therefore, his signature today commands $500 plus, with a signed photograph, which is rarer, selling at $1200 and up. He occasionally did self caricatures which are worth $750 plus, depending on their size. Two or three documents have traded hands in the last couple of years in the $800-1000 range.
**Scarcity Index—★★★★**

**Errol Flynn** (1909-1959)—Errol Flynn's antics offscreen covered as much ink in the tabloids as anything he ever did onscreen, linking him forever with the expression "In Like Flynn." He was undoubtedly the most impressive swashbuckler in tights to ever grace the screen in such classics as *The Adventures of Robin Hood* and *Don Juan*. He was a gracious signer when encountered, but since he neither answered his hordes of fan mail nor had a retirement period to answer mail in, only in-person examples exist of his signature, which runs $350 plus, with signed photographs in the $750 range. Documents and letters are rarer.
**Scarcity Index—★★★★**

**Henry Fonda** (1905-1982)—Henry Fonda was the beginning of an acting dynasty that was carried on by children Jane and Peter. Fonda had a long illustrious career in Hollywood, starring in his first picture in 1929 and winning an Oscar for his last picture, *On Golden Pond*, which also starred daughter Jane, in 1982. It was his second Oscar, having won a Lifetime Achievement Award the year before; he died three months later. With such a long career, which included his occasionally answering his fan mail and signing often when asked in person, his signature has stayed affordable in the $50 range, with signed photographs selling for $150. Letters and documents are scarcer, but have surfaced in the $150 range and up, depending on content.

Scarcity Index—★★

**Glen Ford** (1916-1995)—Starting his career in 1939, Ford interupted it during WWII to serve his country as a Marine. After his military hitch he starred opposite Rita Hayworth in her most famous film *Gilda*. He became a household word, brilliantly playing an inner city teacher in the 1955 classic *Blackboard Jungle*. He is loved by collectors for a variety of western film performances as well. A friendly signer of fan mail in later years, his signature, though, getting uncommon, still sells at around $40, with signed photographs at $100.

Scarcity Index—★★★

**Harrison Ford** (1942-   )—Born July 13, 1942, Harrison Ford has had starring roles in four of the top ten grossing pictures of all time! If he had never starred in any other film but *Star Wars*, he would be collected today as character "Han Solo." However, he also starred as "Indiana Jones" in the hit series of films, and as character "Jack Ryan" in two screen adaptations of the John Clancy novels. He has also given great performances in a re-make of *Sabrina*, *The Fugitive*, and *Blade Runner*. He is a tough signature to obtain, as he does not sign fan mail and is shy in person. He rarely attends parties or galas, and lives in the Midwest—commuting to New York and Los Angeles to do films. His signature sells easily at $75, with signed photographs from *Star Wars* or *Indiana Jones* selling for as much as $300. Documents and letters, as of yet, are scarce.

Scarcity Index—★★★

**William Frawley** (1887-1966)—No matter how many other roles Frawley had (*Miracle on 34th Street*, among others), he will be best remembered as Lucille Ball's neighbor "Fred Mertz," which he played on the TV series from 1951-1960. In person, he was cantankerous towards fans requesting signatures and never signed fan mail, which is why his signature is so scarce, selling at $300 with $500 plus not uncommon on photographs. A document sold last year for $500.

**Scarcity Index—★★★★**

**Clark Gable** (1901-1960)—Gable once told reporters that "the only thing that kept him a big star was the continual re-releasing of the movie *Gone with the Wind* that has introduced me to new audiences each time." He was probably right. To be sure, Gable had a career with many highpoints besides *Gone with the Wind*, but that movie seems to be the reason most collectors desire his signature. His last film in 1961 was *The Misfits* opposite Marilyn Monroe, and many believe the strenuous and extended shooting schedule weakened his health. Three weeks after finishing the film, he died without seeing the great reviews his performance got. He was a friendly signer in person, with his signature selling at $300 plus. About seven years ago, a small trunk was found in one of his old homes that contained approximately 400 canceled personal checks. They are just now beginning to dry up and increase in value, selling for around $450 each. Letters are rare as are documents (other than the aforementioned checks). Signed photographs sell for $700, with an image as "Rhett Butler" bringing twice that amount.

**Scarcity Index—★★★**

**Greta Garbo** (1905-1990)—The most mysterious actress Hollywood has ever produced, who uttered both on and off-screen that "she just wanted to be alone." She was an intensely private celebrity, who never answered mail and only signed occasionally at the height of her fame, and, even more rare, late in her career. She had the opportunity to sign fan mail, but never would. She often wrote friends and signed even these private letters with pen names such as "Harriett Brown" or simply with the initials "GG," such was her thirst for privacy. She was the most expensive celebrity signature for a star that was still living, selling for as much as $1000 while still alive! Since her death, her signature has leveled out around $1200. A very few personal checks have hit the market, and sell for around $3500, as do ANY documents of this rare star. Letters have sold for as much as $10,000! Signed photographs are also very rare, selling for $6000 plus when encountered.
Scarcity Index—★★★★★

**Ava Gardner** (1922-1990)—Gardner never won any acting awards, but by her sheer beauty alone the public made her a star. She had a tempestuous marriage with Frank Sinatra, who many believed loved her like no other woman in his life before or since. She lived the last twenty years of her life retired in Europe only occasionally answering her fan mail. Her signature is worth $60, with photographs selling at $150 plus. Some of her British personal checks have hit the market and sell in the $150 range as well. Memorable films include *Showboat*; *East Side, West Side*; and *The Sun Also Rises*.
Scarcity Index—★★★

**Judy Garland** (1922-1969)—Judy Garland will undoubtedly always be in demand with collectors, which is why her signature continues to rise in value. She was without peer as a singer, and due to her death by overdose, she became a scarcer signature. She will always be collected because she is reintroduced yearly to audiences as "Dorothy" in the classic *The Wizard of Oz*. She died in 1969, and although *Oz* had begun airing on TV in 1956, she did not sign many pictures of herself as Dorothy. Today, collectors find that hard to understand. But at the time of her death, there were not any dealers or collectors who sought stars' signatures, except out of true love for the star, since material gain was not a factor then and a nice portrait is about all a fan could find for her to sign. To find a publicity photograph of *Oz*, which was first released in 1939, was tougher. Her signature varied greatly throughout her career, mainly because of the alcohol and drugs she was often under the influence of. This makes it tricky when buying a signature of hers, and is one of the times that buying from an experienced dealer who offers a Lifetime Guarantee is particularly important. Some checks hit the market a couple of years ago sold by one of her ex-husbands, Sid Luft, with whom she had a daughter. (She also had Liza Minelli with Director Vincent Minelli.) These checks were offered publicly at $800 each. Other documents sell for around $1000 each and her signature alone is worth $400. Signed photographs sell in the $900 range and up. Only two instances of a signed photograph as Dorothy have traded hands in the last few years. In one instance, dealers were divided as to its authenticity and in the other case it sold for $4000. Even rarer are items encountered signed in her real name, Frances Gumm. A document signed in 1936 (three years before she played Dorothy) sold at auction for $2000 last year.
Scarcity Index—★★★

**Greer Garson** (1908-1996)—Perhaps best remembered for an Academy Award-winning performance in the 1942 film *Mrs. Miniver*, Greer Garson was an MGM leading lady for years and adored by audiences. She is collected today by actress and Oscar-winner collectors and having died recently (1996), she is a fairly easy signature to obtain. She signed much of her fan mail in her retirement years as well as when asked in person. A signature runs $30, with a signed photograph at $100. Very few documents or letters have hit the market in the $150 range.
Scarcity Index—★★

**Janet Gaynor** (1906-1984)—Janet Gaynor will always be collected since she was an Oscar winner. In fact, she won the first Best Actress Oscar ever given out, in 1928. She left a body of work most notably in the 1930s and died in 1984. She signed fan mail in her retirement years; therefore, her signature is affordable at $30, with photographs worth $100 plus. Signed letters have hit the market around $100, and documents are rarer. Some of her more memorable films include 1937's *A Star is Born* and *Young at Heart* in 1938.
**Scarcity Index—★★**

**Richard Gere** (1949-    )—Although he had gained some popularity in smaller parts, the 1982 movie, *An Officer and a Gentleman* made Gere a star. Years later, *Pretty Woman* would insure his continued success in films, although his personal life was tougher. His marriage to supermodel Cindy Crawford ending in 1995. Gere is not a willing signer in public. In fact, his signature sells for $40 when you can find one, and rarer photographs sell for $100 and up. A few documents have sold in the $250 range. We can only hope that he will loosen up his signing habits soon.
**Scarcity Index—★★★**

**Lillian Gish** (1893-1993)—Lillian Gish was the top female box office star during the silent era. When her first talkie film flopped (not due to her abilities) she went to Broadway. She won a special Lifetime Achievement Oscar in 1971. Incredibly, she never married, but was always close to her actress/sister Dorothy, who died in 1968. Lillian died in 1993, and for many of her last years in retirement answered a prodigious amount of fan mail. She often signed "In remembrance, Lillian Gish," and such a signature sells today for $30, with photographs selling for $60 plus.
**Scarcity Index—★**

**Jackie Gleason** (1916-1987)—On TV, Gleason created such timeless characters as "Ralph Kramden" and "Reggie Van Gleason" on "The Honeymooners." He was nicknamed by his peers "The Great One" and was deserving of the adulation. He did as well in drama as comedy, which he proved in 1961 with an Academy Award nomination for *The Hustler*. One interesting note is that he was afraid of flying and preferred to live in Florida—the complete opposite coast from Hollywood where so much of his work required him to be. But he was a big enough star to always require production companies to wait the three days it would take for him to travel by train. He often referred to these trips as "Party Trains," because he would bring friends and often a small Jazz band to play cards, music, and have as drinking buddies during the trips coast to coast. In his retired years, he often signed fan mail, but demand has caused his signature to continue to rise in price, currently at $75, with signed photographs at $200. (Most collected are "The Honeymooners" or *Smokey and the Bandit* images.) A few letters and documents have sold in the $200 range as well.
**Scarcity Index—★★**

**Paulette Goddard** (1911-1990)—Goddard had only done bit parts in films when she met Charlie Chaplin at a party. They were soon wed. He cast her in better movies, which launched her career. She divorced him in 1942 and later married Burgess Meredith. She was always a willing signer in person and had intermittently signed her fan mail, keeping her signature price fairly steady at $30, with photographs at around $100. She died in 1990. Some of her more memorable film roles were *Modern Times* and *The Great Dictator* opposite Chaplin. Director David O'Selznik once said that he would have chosen her to play "Scarlett" in *Gone with the Wind*, but was afraid of a public outcry if he did because of her "untraditional" wedding on board a yacht at sea with Chaplin.
**Scarcity Index—★★**

**Betty Grable** (1916-1973)—Grable was dubbed America's pinup during World War II (pre-Monroe days), with her famous legs always the focal point of each shot. In fact, a now-infamous publicity stunt was insuring her legs for $1 million. She starred in several films and enjoyed a long career in Hollywood as a top female box office draw. Many Marilyn Monroe fans collect her signature as the third woman (along with Monroe and Lauren Bacall), in the classic *How to Marry a Millionaire* in 1953. She died of cancer in 1973. She signed fan mail some in her retirement years, and in person for her fans. Her  signature is getting less common, however, and currently runs $100 with photographs in the $250 range. Letters are prevalent, although often only signed "Betty," which hurts their value. Documents are the most uncommon form of her signature.

**Scarcity Index—★★★**

**Cary Grant** (1904-1986)—Grant rated at the top of male box office draws for over twenty years in a long successful career, in films like *Gunga Din* in 1939 to Hitchcock classics like *To Catch a Thief* opposite Grace Kelly. Most people remember him in the classic *An Affair to Remember* or *North by Northwest,* and the comedy classic *Operation Petticoat* with Tony Curtis. One of the most impersonated stars due to his unique voice and delivery, no Hollywood collection is complete without him. Although he had a long career and signed in person for his fans, he rarely signed fan mail, due to its high volume and his popularity throughout his career. He died in 1986 but rarely signed after retiring in 1970 (the same year he received a special Lifetime Achievement Oscar). His signature sells for $250, with a photograph bringing $500. A few letters and documents have sold in the $500 range as well.

**Scarcity Index—★★★**

**Hugh Grant** (1960-   )—I guess we will never know if Grant's performances alone would have driven him so quickly to stardom or was it the "incident" with Divine Brown one fateful night in Hollywood. (She has since written a book about it and he publically apologized on David Letterman's and Jay Leno's shows.) It was fortuitous that it happened just prior to the release of his movie *Nine Months*. He has gone on to other solid performances in films such as *The Englishman Who Went Up a Hill* and *Sense and Sensibility*. Time will tell if he goes down in history as a great actor or a scandal in the public's mind. A signature is currently worth $25, with signed photographs at $50.
Scarcity Index—★★

**Alec Guiness** (1914-   )—One of the classically trained British actors whose accomplishments have gotten him knighted by the Queen, making him Sir Alec Guiness. He won an Oscar for his performance in the *Bridge on the River Kwai*. But if not collected as an Oscar winner, he is most assuredly collected as "Obi Wan Kenobi" in *Star Wars*. It is as Obi Wan Kenobi that he is most collected on signed photographs at around $60, with his signature at $25. He retired to his home in England which has made his signature a little tougher to obtain. Thankfully, he signed fan mail for several years until the last couple, when old age seems to have slowed him down. Other memorable films include *Lawrence of Arabia*, *Doctor Zhivago*, and *Murder by Death*. He won a Lifetime Achievement Oscar in 1980.
Scarcity Index—★

**Jack Haley** (1898-1979)—He first came to fame starring opposite Shirley Temple in *Rebecca of Sunnybrook Farm*, and again in *Poor Little Rich Girl*. But, of course, he yearly delights audiences as the "Tin Man" in the classic *The Wizard of Oz*. He was always a friendly signer for fans, even appearing at a few *Oz* conventions prior to his death. His widow is still alive today and owns his original prop oil can from the film! His signature sells for $900, with signed portraits at $150. Signed photographs as the Tin Man sell for $300 plus. Some personal and business checks have hit the market and are currently selling in the $150 range. The personal checks are much scarcer than the ones drawn on his business account, "Madeira."
Scarcity Index—★★★

**Margaret Hamilton** (1902-1985)—You may remember her from all of those coffee commercials she did in her retirement years as "Cora," but schoolteacher-turned-character actress Hamilton will go down in collecting history as the "Wicked Witch of the West" from the classic *The Wizard of Oz*. Until her death in 1985, she generously signed fan mail, although she often  signed photographs with her nickname "Maggie," or merely her initials; these are worth considerbly less than a full signature. A signature alone sells at $100, with signed "Wicked Witch" photographs selling at $300. A few documents and handwritten letters have surfaced selling for $400 plus. She often signed "WWW" for "Wicked Witch of the West" after her name.
**Scarcity Index—★★**

**Tom Hanks** (1956-   )—Hanks is a friendly signer (he should be since he has a lot to be thankful for with fans). Most comedians who have success on a TV series as he did with "Bosom Buddies," rarely become A-list movie stars. Not only is he a huge movie star, he did what only actor Spencer Tracy had done before him, which was win back to back Oscars for *Philadelphia* and *Forest Gump*. Many thought he was going to do it again for *Apollo 13*. *Philadelphia* is not a collectible photographic image, however, probably because of its grave subject matter. Instead, most collectors pay $100 and up for photographs of him as "Forest Gump" or from *Apollo 13*. A signature sells for $40. No documents or letters have hit the market as of yet, but given time, some should appear.
**Scarcity Index—★★★**

**Jean Harlow** (1911-1937)—One of the most expensive of the Hollywood legends to collect, Harlow led a tragic personal life that ended too soon. But on the screen she began the public's fascination with the platinum blonde long before Monroe. It was Howard Hughes that gave her the biggest break by starring her in the film *Hell's Angels*, which was one of the top ten films of the year. She became ill while filming *Saratoga* in 1937 and died of uraemic poisoning. Many believe her mother would not take her to a doctor soon enough due to her religious beliefs. Very often her manager and overprotective mother signed for her, including all of her fan mail, making her authentic signature quite rare. So beware of getting a "Mama Harlow" instead of the real thing. Her authentic signature sells for $1200, with photographs selling for $2500 and up. Documents and letters are even rarer.
Scarcity Index—★★★★★

**Rex Harrison** (1908-1990)—Classy and sophisticated, Harrison was the very British star of such classics as *My Fair Lady* and *Dr. Doolittle*. (Hepburn played "Eliza Doolittle" in *My Fair Lady*—strange that the uncommon name would appear again in his career—makes one superstitious a bit, eh?) In 1989, he was knighted and given the title "Sir" by her Majesty the Queen. He was playing in a British stage revival of *My Fair Lady* when he died of cancer. He was a gracious signer for fans in person and signed quite a bit of his fan mail in his later years. His signature is getting a bit more uncommon, but is still available for around $40, with signed photographs from his most famous two roles selling at $150.
Scarcity Index—★★

**Susan Hayward** (1918-1975)—A great American name for a glamorous actress who was born Edythe Marriner (no one ever thought her name change was a bad idea) and started as a model before breaking into films. She won an Oscar in 1958 for *I Want To Live*. But tragically, she died of cancer in 1975. She is a fairly scarce autograph, as most stars are that have untimely or unexpected deaths, with her signature selling for $200, and photographs at $450. Other memorable film roles include *The Fighting SeeBees*, *Valley of the Dolls*, and *Rawhide*.
Scarcity Index—★★★★

**Rita Hayworth** (1918-1987)—Ravishing Rita Hayworth played and danced opposite the great male leads of the time, including Gene Kelly, Fred Astaire, and Jimmy Cagney. Magazine reporters loved her (she made the cover of *Life* magazine twice). The 1946 film *Gilda* is considered a classic by many, and no Hollywood actress collection would be complete without her. Sadly, by 1977, she was an alcoholic and being treated for  Alzheimer's disease. She died in 1987 in her daughter's care. Due to the obvious ravages of the disease, she was unable to answer fan mail in her retirement years, even if she had been willing. Her signature sells for $150 plus, with photographs around $350. Some documents have surfaced recently in the $350 range as well. Memorable film roles include *You'll Never Get Rich* and *Pal Joey*.
**Scarcity Index—★★★**

**Audrey Hepburn** (1929-1993)—If Hepburn had not wanted a career in film, she could have been a great runway model, with her tiny frame and stunning good looks. She starred in only a handful of films, but most are considered classics today. *Breakfast at Tiffany's*, *GiGi*, and *My Fair Lady* are just three. She retired early and lived abroad the rest of her life, doing work in third world countries caring for the hungry. She died far too young, of cancer, in 1993. Fortunately for her fans, when she visited New York City, she often signed dozens of dealers' photographs, most depicting her in her most collected image as "Eliza Doolittle" in *My Fair Lady*. These photographs bring $250 currently, with her signature worth $100. Only a couple of documents have surfaced so far, and have sold in the $500 range.
**Scarcity Index—★★★**

**Katherine Hepburn** (1907-  )—Surely one of the top legendary performers, male or female, Miss Hepburn is a must for Oscar collectors and any serious collection of Hollywood stars. Born in 1907, her career starred her opposite Spencer Tracy, Humphrey Bogart, and many other top leading men. In fact, we could fill a book just discussing her amazing career. But we'll concentrate, instead, on her rather strange signing habits. Her career began at RKO in the mid 1930s, and, as a new starlet, she would sign for people she met as well as the occasional photograph. But when she became established by the early 1940s, she would begin a lifelong aversion to signing photographs. (She feels she is unattractive.) She has been steadfast in this rule of hers and many signed photographs after the 1940s are fakes, especially those signed with her now trademark shaky handwriting (a medical condition she has had for the last 15 years). Her shakiness has gotten so bad in the last two years, she now has her mail signed by an autopen (mechanical device) and secretaries, so BE CAREFUL of any typed letters signed after early 1993. These familiar small typed notes on her red stationery are what are most often encountered in the market today, with normal content (brief remarks) signed in full, bringing $250. (Bear in mind she is still alive.) You should not pay as much for notes signed "Kate" or "K. Hepburn." Signatures on anything other than these letters are scarce, as she has never liked to sign in person. A signature alone is worth $150. The few vintage-signed photographs that do come to market sell for $1000 due to their rarity. She has signed the covers of many playbills during her Broadway work, and handwritten letters have hit the market (usually to friends and signed simply "Kate") that sell for $400 and up, depending on content. A small amount of uncashed checks were sold by one man (approx. 8) that were quickly gobbled up at around $550 each, and a few other documents have surfaced that sell in that same range.

**Scarcity Index—★★**

**Charlton Heston** (1924-   )—Heston has had quite a knack at starring in some of the most popular films of all time. He is collected on signed photographs primarily from *Planet of the Apes* and as "Moses" from the *The Ten Commandments*, but has certainly starred in many others. He has signed his fan mail now for years, making his signature the most plentiful of any actors' (next to "Batman's" Adam West, but I digress). In fact, one autograph dealer who tries to get authentic signatures from retired stars in the mail, once said that Heston signs so many and so fast for him and other autograph collectors, that they expect signatures to be arriving in their mailbox weeks after his death! His signature sells for about $15, with the aforementioned photographs selling for around $30. Checks of Heston's have also hit the market at around $30, as well as letters.
Scarcity Index—★

**Dustin Hoffman** (1937-   )—This Oscar-winning method actor has a great body of work for fans to watch and he shows no sign of slowing. From *The Graduate* to *Midnight Cowboy*, *Kramer Vs. Kramer*, and *Rain Man*, Hoffman has played dozens of roles brilliantly, including a woman in *Tootsie*! A signed photograph sells for $60, with a signature selling at $30. Few documents and letters exist on the market so far. (The most popular images are as "Hook" from *Peter Pan*, *Tootsie* in drag, and the *Rain Man*.)
Scarcity Index—★★

**Bob Hope** (1903-   )—Off and on for years, Bob Hope has signed "Thanks for the Memories" (his trademark song) on photographs. Unfortunately, so did his secretary of 35 years, whom, he has admitted publicly, signed nearly all of his fan mail for him during that time. The best way to get an authentic Hope is from a dealer or collector who obtained it in person, that is, witnessed him signing it.
His signature is actually sloppier than hers. A few documents have surfaced in the $150 range, which are good to collect, too. He has signed in person when asked, until these past couple of years when age and failing eyesight has finally stopped him (he is, after all, 95 years old). The proliferation of his secretary's signature on the market with his has kept the price of a signature reasonable, at around $35, with photographs at $100, but be sure you are getting an authentic one for your collection.

Scarcity Index—★★

**Leslie Howard** (1893-1943)—Often playing the staid Englishman in pictures, Howard will always be remembered (and collected) for playing one of the major roles in *Gone with the Wind* in 1939. He was killed in 1943 after his plane was shot down while near enemy lines on his way to lecture on the ongoing war. Dying so soon after his most famous role, his signed photographs in character are non-existent, with the few signed portraits of him selling for between $550 and $700. His signature alone sells for $300, with documents and letters quite scarce. With more people collecting the *GWTW* cast with each passing year, the finite number of his signatures is being gobbled up, causing the price to continually rise.
**Scarcity Index—★★★★**

**Rock Hudson** (1925-1985)—Always playing the romantic leading man, many fans were shocked to find out he was dying of AIDS that he contracted from a homosexual lifestyle. He is most remembered for his comedies opposite Doris Day, although he turned in a great performance late in his career opposite Liz Taylor in the 1980 Agatha Christie adaptation, *The Mirror Cracked*. He died in 1985. He had been (fortunately for his fans) a friendly signer throughout his career with his signature selling now for $60, and a signed photograph at $100. A few documents have surfaced selling in the $150-200 range, as have a few typed letters. Other memorable film roles include *Ice Station Zebra*, *Winchester '73*, and *Pillow Talk*.
**Scarcity Index—★★**

**Kim Hunter** (1922-    )—Born in 1922, Hunter should be remembered as being the "Stella" that Brando was screaming about in *A Streetcar Named Desire*, for which she won an Academy Award. Yet her most collected image is unrecognizable as the sympathetic ape scientist that kisses Charleton Heston in the sci-fi classic *Planet of the Apes*. Signed "Ape" photographs sell at $40, with her signature at $15, due to her generous signing habits by mail and in person for fans. She often signed a great image of her kissing Heston in the first movie of the series (*Planet of the Apes*), which is then often signed by Heston himself. Signed by both, it can be purchased for around $75. She is a part-owner of the new theme restaurant chain called The Fashion Cafe.
**Scarcity Index—★**

**Kathy Ireland** (1963-    )—According to most sources who have worked over the years photographing this Sports Illustrated lovely, she is the nicest to work with of all the super-models. Her pinup photographs sell for $60, and a signature at $25. She has signed mail in the past, but currently does not, probably due to increased demands on her time. Documents and letters are currently scarce, too, but in time may hit the market.
Scarcity Index—★

**Michael Jackson** (1958-    )—The self-proclaimed King of Pop is notoriously reclusive, making his signature scarce. A signed photograph sells for $350, with a signature at $150. A few documents have hit the market in the $1000 plus range. Letters are scarcer. He has signed quite a few fedoras (like he wore in several videos) and given them to charity auctions. Many have then found their way back into the autograph market and sell for around $1200 each. (Interestingly, they are all dated 1998—no one is sure why.) He also did a signed limited edition gold record award copy in a frame for an autograph company that sold for $450 wholesale. It sold out and retails at around $600 currently. His rather tarnished image (with alleged misconduct charges with youths) has hurt the value and demand on his signature, but there can be no doubt he has left his mark on popular music.
Scarcity Index—★★★★

**Al Jolson** (1886-1950)—Jolson was one of the very few legendary vaudeville performers to make the jump to the silver screen. He had a great singing style (and great ego concerning it) and sold record numbers of albums, as well as theater tickets. He once said that he believed ego was a virtue! He will always be remembered as the first star of the talkies when he starred in *The Jazz Singer* in 1927. He seemed to make every social party and signed for fans at all of them, which has kept his signature fairly affordable at $150, with a signed photograph running $400. A signed photograph in blackface, which was how he often sang his signature hit "Mammy," is rarer and worth about $700 when encountered. Documents have sold in the $500 range, as have letters.
Scarcity Index—★★★

**Jennifer Jones** (1919-    )—In 1949, Jones married mogul David O'Selznik and her career (not surprisingly) took off.  When Selznik died in 1965, she retired, although she did do a few minor films. She lives in California, but absolutely hates signing autographs, and will not do so when approached. Even the few letters that have sold on the market were usually signed simply "Jennifer." Her signature is scarce enough that it is currently priced at $150, with signed photographs at $350. Memorable films include *A Farewell to Arms* and *Tender is the Night*.
Scarcity Index—★★★★

**Victor Jory** (1902-1982)—Victor Jory may not have been easily recognized on the street, as many character actors weren't, but he starred in over 120 films! He is most collected today for having starred in the 1939 classic, *Gone with the Wind*. He signed at the height of his career when approached by fans, but sporadically in retirement years, making his signature uncommon. It sells at $50, with signed photographs at $150. Other memorable film roles include *A MidSummer Night's Dream* and *The Fugitive Kind*.
**Scarcity Index—★★★**

**Boris Karloff** (1887-1969)—One of the kings of the horror screen, Karloff was a great actor, and master of makeup as well. He starred in *Frankenstein*, *The Mummy*, *The Bride of Frankenstein*, and many other classic Universal horror pictures. Many people are not aware that he was the narrator for the classic cartoon, "The Grinch who Stole Christmas," which has played as a yearly yuletide classic on TV for over twenty years. Karloff was always a friendly signer in person, but rarely signed fan mail. His signature sells for $300, with photographs running $550 (portraits). However, signed photographs in one of his horror roles such as "Frankenstein" or the "The Mummy" sell for $1000 and up. Letters have hit the market in the $400 range, and a few with extraordinary content (describing his experiences on the set of *Frankenstein*, for example) have sold as high as $1500. Several documents have sold in the past few years in the $500-700 range, each dealing with TV and stage appearances.
**Scarcity Index—★★★**

**Buster Keaton** (1895-1966)—The "great stoneface," as Keaton was nicknamed, is considered to this day one of comedy's great geniuses. He did most of the writing, producing, and directing in each of his films and ALL of the stunts—many of which were as spectacular as they were dangerous. He preferred to work silently, with just a wink or a stare conveying a wide range of emotions. Adding Keaton along with Charlie Chaplin, Harold Lloyd, and Fatty Arbuckle, you would have a collection of the pioneers in film comedy. Keaton died in 1966 and is a fairly scarce signature today valued at $250, with photographs selling at $500. Documents and letters are even rarer. He came out of retirement to appear in the classic romp *It's a Mad, Mad, Mad, Mad World*, and won an Oscar for Lifetime Achievement in 1959.
**Scarcity Index—★★★★**

**Michael Keaton** (1951-    )—Keaton is best-known in comedies such as *Mr. Mom* and *Beetlejuice*, although he turned in a great dramatic performance in *Clean and Sober*. But it is as "Batman" in 1989, and again in *Batman Returns* in 1992 that collectors most desire signed photographs, which bring $75. Single signatures are worth $30. Documents and letters are scarcer thus far, but it is still early in his career. He is a friendly signer in person, although he has not as of yet signed fan mail.
**Scarcity Index—★★**

**Ruby Keeler** (1909-1993)—Ruby Keeler started and spent most of her career in the silent era with only a couple of talkie films. Although she made a handful of TV appearances in the thirty odd years following her last film in 1938, she stayed pretty much retired from the 1940s until her death. She was always a friendly signer and signed her fan mail for years before her death, keeping her signature affordable at $20, with signed photographs at $50. She owed her start as a dancer in early Busby Berkley films to her husband, actor/singer Al Jolson. However, he also held her career back from what it could have been.
**Scarcity Index—★★**

**Gene Kelly** (1912-1996)—One of the greatest dancers in cinema history—and a great actor and director as well—Kelly danced with an animated mouse, Fred Astaire, Debbie Reynolds, Donald O'Connor, and Olivia Newton John, to name but a few. He directed Barbra Streisand in *Hello Dolly*, and will forever be remembered for his innovative dance numbers in the classic *Singing in the Rain*. (Perched on the lamp post is the most collected photograph image of his career.) A signed portrait sells for $65, but the classic *Singing in the Rain* images sell for more ($125) with his signature at $40. He signed much of his fan mail the last years of his retirement before being incapacitated by several strokes that eventually claimed his life in 1996. He has used secretaries to sign, especially after his first stroke, so you must be careful buying a Kelly signature. A few documents have sold for $200 and up, as have some letters.
**Scarcity Index—★★**

**Grace Kelly** (1929-1982)— Many actresses have played princesses, but Grace Kelly actually became one when she married Prince Rainier. She had a fairy tale wedding and returned to her kingdom in Monaco, where she retired as an actress. She had already become a famous star in such films as *High Society* when she married Rainier. When she retired as an actress, if she was ever asked to sign for a fan, she signed her proper name of "Grace DeMonaco," not Kelly. For this reason, when she died in 1982 at such a young age, collectors began to realize that the Grace Kelly version of her signature was rarer than the Grace DeMonaco version. After all, she was Grace Kelly when she acted, so the market prices for the two forms of her signature began to separate with a DeMonaco signature now selling for  $175, and a Grace Kelly signature selling at $250, with the respective photographs selling for $250, and $500. Documents are scarce, but quite a few letters were sold at auction a year ago for top money (in the $750 and up range), many of which were only signed "Grace," but had great content and were handwritten.
**Scarcity Index—as Grace Kelly ★★★★**
**as Grace DeMonaco ★★★**

**Evelyn Keyes** (1919-    )—Born in 1919, Keyes never could get her performances out of the supporting class into starring roles. She put in solid performances in many films but mostly forgettable subject matter UNTIL she played "Scarlett O'Hara's" younger sister "Sue Ellen" in *Gone with the Wind*, a role for which she will always be remembered. During her heyday, she tore up the gossip pages, however. Her first husband shot himself after their divorce. She married director Charles Vidor, but left him for director John Huston, whom she divorced after four years. She lived on again, off again with producer Mike Todd and in 1957, married bandleader Artie Shaw. She has been a friendly signer of her fan mail for several years now, which has kept photographs of her as "Sue Ellen" affordable at $50, and signatures at $20, but at her passing, these are sure to increase in value.
**Scarcity Index—★★**

**Val Kilmer** (1959-    )—Kilmer has suffered from good press and bad in what has been a short but meteoric rise to fame. Who knew when he played in the sophomoric film *Real Genius* that in a short span of time he would be working with DeNiro and Pacino (*Heat*) or get $10 million to play "Batman" (replacing Michael Keaton) or star opposite screen legend Marlon Brando (*Island of Dr. Moreau*). Like him or not, he is a screen presence that appears to be here to stay, and he is already collectible—especially on photographs depicting him from the movie *Tombstone*, as "Jim Morrison" in *The Doors*, and of course, as "Batman." He doesn't currently sign fan mail, but he is a friendly signer when approached in person. He also signed a limited edition *Batman* image that was sold in the Warner Brothers retail stores at $600 (limited to 750). But, fortunately, you can locate an authentic signed photograph for around $100, or a signature for $40. Documents and letters have not surfaced as of yet. But who knows what the future will hold for Val? In 1995, he divorced his wife and entered single life yet again.
**Scarcity Index—★★**

**Alan Ladd** (1913-1964)—One of the all-time great tough guys in over 50 films, Alan Ladd is best remembered in the 1949 film *The Great Gatsby* and 1953's *Shane*. Incredibly, he turned down the lead in the film *Giant*, which would go to James Dean and make him a star. Tragically, he died of an alcohol/drug overdose in 1964. (He had been a heavy drinker for years prior.) A signature will cost $75 currently, with a signed photograph fetching $200.
**Scarcity Index**—★★★

**Bert Lahr** (1895-1967)—Starting as a performer in circuses as a clown, Lahr never would be a cinematic success. However, he nonetheless secured a place for himself in cinema history when he played the "Cowardly Lion" in *The Wizard of Oz*. Due to his death so many years ago, Oz photographs are almost unheard of. However, regular signed photographs of Lahr sell for around $550, as do the few documents that have surfaced. A signature alone brings $300. An interesting side note is that the costume he wore as the Cowardly Lion was made from a real lion's pelt and weighed 40 pounds, with inside tempera-tures often rising over 100 degrees while Lahr was required to work in it. One custume that sold at an MGM auction in 1970 for $3200 changed hands privately last year for $100,000!
**Scarcity Index**—★★★★

**Hedy Lamarr** (1913-    )—Hedy was considered one of the most beautiful women on the screen at the time. She is best remem-bered as the temptress "Delilah" in the 1949 classic *Samson and Delilah*. Married six times, she retired from filmmaking in 1966, and lives rather reclusively in Florida. She has signed fan mail sporadically for years, keeping her signature reasonable at $30, with a photograph at $100. Other memorable film roles include *Tortilla Flat* and *Let's Live a Little*.
**Scarcity Index**—★★

**Burt Lancaster** (1910-1994)—A legendary leading male actor, Burt Lancaster will be remembered for many roles like "Elmer Gantry" in 1960, for which he assured his collectibility by winning an Oscar. He also turned in a great performance as the "Birdman" in *Birdman of Alcatraz* in 1962. He retired from acting at age 77, and died in 1994 at age 80. He signed some fan mail in the last few years of his life, and his signature currently sells for $60, with a signed photograph selling for $125. Other memorable film roles include *Gunfight at the OK Corral*, *Run Silent, Run Deep*, and *Field of Dreams*.
**Scarcity Index**—★★

**Carole Landis** (1919-1948)—*A Star is Born* and *A Day at the Races* were just a couple of the movies this blonde bombshell quickly landed roles in. But on her breathless climb to the top she kept letting her personal life, which was in bad repair, affect her career. It caused her to never climb out as more than a supporting actress status and to go through four marriages before she was 29! At age 30, feeling spurned by her married lover, actor Rex Harrison, she committed suicide. Therefore, her signature is quite scarce today, and sells at $125, with signed photographs at $250.
**Scarcity Index**—★★★★

**Charles Laughton** (1899-1962)—One of the greatest screen actors in the history of film, Laughton played an incredibly wide range of characters from "Nero" to "Capt. Bligh." He was married to actress Elsa Lanchester (*The Bride of Frankenstein*) and he passed away from cancer in 1962. He is collected for those in search of all of the Oscar winners, and as a great actor in his own right. His signature looks careless, but not unlike an indecipherable doctor's signature. Laughton's consistently looked this way. Documents and letters are scarcer, but his signature alone runs $100, with signed photographs at $250. Memorable film roles include *The Hunchback of Notre Dame*, *Mutiny on the Bounty*, and *Captain Kidd*.
**Scarcity Index**—★★★

**Laurel and Hardy** (1890-1965 and 1890-1957)—One of the greatest comedy teams of all time, Laurel and Hardy are always heavily requested signatures from autograph dealers, partly because they are famous worldwide. Their mannerisms are still impersonated by comedians today with the thin, always bumbling Stan Laurel upsetting his portly partner Oliver Hardy. During the height of their fame, teams of secretaries handled their mail, signing the names themselves or sending out rubber-stamped and printed photographs. When you do find a photograph signed by them both it will rarely ever be inscribed by Hardy, but often is inscribed by Stan. It will usually be the more economical 5" x 7" size, which today sells for around $800. A rarer sized 8" x 10" photograph could bring $1500. The pairs' signatures on the same album page or piece of paper commands around $750, but a little less if on two separate pieces. Individually, Stan Laurel's signature is worth $200 with Oliver Hardy's signature at $350. Laurel corresponded over the years with many fans and acquaintances, and his typed letters sell often in the $300-400 range if signed in full; he often signed only "Stan" however, and these letters bring less.

**Scarcity Index—Stan Laurel ★★★ Oliver Hardy ★★★★**
**Both Together ★★★★**

**Peter Lawford** (1923-1984)—Lawford was a good actor, but never broke through to greatness onscreen. Offscreen, his exploits are more remembered—first as a member of Sinatra's "Rat Pack," for which he is collected today, and for the social circles he ran in after marrying Patricia Kennedy in 1954. He is said to have been the first on the scene of Marilyn Monroe's death, even being called before police or ambulance crews. He was the one who first arranged for President John Kennedy to meet the star.

**Scarcity Index—★★★**

**Brandon Lee** (1965-1993)—Brandon Lee (son of Bruce Lee) was filming what would have become his breakout movie, *The Crow*, when a prop person "accidentally" switched real bullets into a prop gun instead of blanks. The actor who fired at young Brandon Lee did so in the scene at point blank range, killing him almost instantly. Sadly, this sort of tragedy was fodder for one gruesome press release after another, which started rumors that he, like his father, was murdered. (No evidence supports either claim.) But it has made him a collectible signature and a very rare one at that. His lawyer's office, which represented him in movie negotiations, sold approximately 35 endorsed checks to dealers, who quickly sold out of them in the $500 and up range. One document for a movie he was in sold shortly after his death for $1750. His signature sells in the $350 range, with signed photographs selling for $600.

**Scarcity Index—★★★★★**

**Bruce Lee** (1940-1973)—Without question, Lee did more to make people want to take martial arts lessons than anyone before or since. His movies *Game of Death* and *Enter the Dragon* are classics in the martial arts genre, and his tragic death at the height of his career caused his signature to rise rapidly in price. He is rare enough as a signature, selling for $400, but photographs are rarer still, selling at $900 and up. Those picturing him as "Kato," the part he played on the TV series "Green Hornet," are worth even more. His family sold many letters and personal items of his at auction, with the average price of a letter being $1700 plus. They also sold to dealers approximately 130 personal checks signed by him, which currently run in the $800 plus range.

**Scarcity Index—★★★★**

**Christopher Lee** (1922- )—Lee remains, as of this writing, the only living legend of horror films unless you allow the mantle to pass to Robert Englund. His predecessors like Lugosi, Chaney, and Karloff have all passed away, and his contemporaries Cushing, and Vincent Price, have passed away as well. Lee has played "Dracula" in more films than any other actor. In fact, the bloodier Hammer-directed films of the 1960s and 1970s he played in, many believe made the way for the gorier horror films of today, such as the *Nightmare*, *Halloween*, and *Jason* movies. He lives in England and sporadically signed his fan mail in the past, but has not in some time, reputedly due to health problems. He is also collected on photographs as "Scaramunga," the villain in the James Bond picture *The Man with the Golden Gun*, as well as on as "Dracula" photographs. Either of these photographs currently sell for $100, but will probably soar in value after his death. A signature sells for $35.
Scarcity Index—★★

**Vivien Leigh** (1913-1967)—Even had she not played the one part for which she is collected today, Vivien Leigh would probably still be collected as a great actress. She married a legendary actor, Laurence Olivier, and often signed letters "Vivien Olivier." She will always be collected for playing "Scarlett O'Hara" in *Gone with the Wind*. Her signature still rises in value and is currently running $350, with signed portraits selling for around $600, but if the photograph is as Scarlett, it will fetch $1500 easily. Her typed letters sell in the $550 range, as do documents. Other memorable film roles include *Anna Karenina* and *Caesar and Cleopatra*.
Scarcity Index—★★★

**Jack Lemmon** (1925- )—Jack Lemmon is one of those great actors that seems to be in all of the classic movies. He played in the movie version of the *The Odd Couple*, which launched the TV series that ran for years. He was Oscar-nominated for movies such as the *The China Syndrome* and is collected, along with actor Tony Curtis, for his hilarious drag playing role opposite Marilyn Monroe, in *Some Like It Hot*. He has always been generous answering fan mail and signs willingly in person, keeping his signature reasonable at $15, with signed photographs at $40. Documents and letters have sold in the $75 range. Other memorable roles include *Mister Roberts*, *Grumpy Old Men*, and *The Apartment*.
Scarcity Index—★

**Jerry Lewis** (1926-    )—Not always a friendly signer in person, but a great signer of his fan mail, collectors can pick from some great signed images, such as *The Nutty Professor*, or photographs signed with longtime partner Dean Martin (deceased). A signed photograph sells for $30, with a signature at $15. Lewis still appears in plays as well as hosting his annual Muscular Dystrophy Telethon, and lives in Las Vegas, Nevada.
Scarcity Index—★

**Harold Lloyd** (1893-1971)—With Keaton and Chaplin, Lloyd is the last of the silent Kings of Comedy. His most famous film has him hanging from a large outdoor clock in an image most will remember (and a stunt he accomplished long before the advent of trick photography). He won a special Oscar in 1962, and was always a willing signer as well as signing fan mail in his retired years. His signature sells for $100, with a photograph selling at $300. Approximately 40 of his vintage personal checks hit the market three years ago and now sell for $200 each.
Scarcity Index—★★★

**Sophia Loren** (1934-    )—Even in her 60s Sophia still looked great in the film *Grumpier Old Men* (1995). From her beginning in the 1957 film, *Boy on a Dolphin*, as a peasant diver looking for archaeological treasures, she always played the sexy siren role. In fact, one of the most collected photographs of her is the shot in this film where she has just gotten out of the water. She won a Best Actress Oscar along the way, making her a must for Oscar collectors as well. She has always lived abroad, but has, for years, signed photographs and cards sent to her by fans, keeping her signature reasonable at $20, with photographs at $50.
Scarcity Index—★

**Peter Lorre** (1904-1964)—Lorre is one of the screen's best villains, with as unique a vocal delivery as any star ever had. With a look and a word or two, he could send shivers. As with many character actors, he rarely was recognized out in public, so he didn't sign much for fans. Nor did he sign much fan mail, which, considering the reasons there are to collect him, has had demand outstripping supply for quite a while now. He starred in the classic film *Casablanca* as well as *The Maltese Falcon,* and had a memorable performance in Disney's classic *20,000 Leagues Under The Sea.* He died in 1964, making his signature uncommon today, selling at $200, with a signed photograph worth $400. (More if from *Casablanca*). A few documents have surfaced selling for around $500.
**Scarcity Index—★★★★**

**Bela Lugosi** (1884-1956)—Hungarian-born Bela Lugosi first played the role that would shape his career—"Dracula"—in the 1920s on Broadway. When Lon Chaney, Sr., died before he could play the part on film, they cast Lugosi instead. He is more identified with the role than any other actor to this day. He was addicted to drugs and squandered his money (and, as it turned out, his health) which kept him from being offered any roles, except those sinister and dark characters similiar in scope to the famous vampire. Young director Ed Wood became his friend during his last years and employed him in several of his B horror movies that are considered classics today—because they are so bad! It was in Wood's most famous (or infamous) movie *Planet Nine from Outerspace* that Lugosi died while filming. By the way, it is true that he was buried (per his personal instructions), in the cape he wore in the film version of Dracula. (If only Planet Hollywood existed 40 years ago he could have sold the cape for enough money to not have died penniless, as he did). His wife signed MOST of his fan mail and although differences in their respective signatures are subtle, a trained eye can tell one from the other. BE CAREFUL that you are buying his signature and not hers! He rarely signed the word "Dracula," usually signing "Sincerely" or "In Remembrance," instead, above his name. A signature is worth $350 plus, with a signed portrait at $1500. A signed photograph as Dracula sells for $3500 easily. Only a couple of documents have sold in the past few years, selling in the $2000 plus range. A handwritten letter mentioning his famous role sold for $2500 last year.
**Scarcity Index—★★★★**

**Paul Lukas** (1895-1971)—Needed for any Academy Award collection, Paul Lukas started his career in the silent days of the cinema, but made the transition to the talkies with relative ease. Unfortunately, he had a reputation for being difficult to work with, which hurt his career by the mid-1940s. Many think, though, that one of his best film roles was as the "Professor" in the 1954 Disney classic *20,000 Leagues Under the Sea*. He died in 1971. His signature can be found with a little looking on the part of the collector, and sells for $50, with photographs selling at $100.
**Scarcity Index—★★★**

**Madonna** (1959-   )—Few superstars are aware that their signature even has value at all let alone what exactly that value is. Madonna is VERY aware and rarely signs for just this reason. It's working so far, with her signature currently selling at $200, with a signed photograph selling in excess of $500. Some documents have traded hands at $1000 when on the market. She has definitely left her mark on the music scene, and continues to try to do the same on film, but she is still fairly young, and years away from retirement. She may begin signing more for fans, which makes buying her signature now a risky investment. However, I would have said the same thing about Buddy Holly or James Dean at the height of their careers. So it really is up to the individual collector. Film highlights include *Who's That Girl?*, *Dick Tracy*, and *Evita*.
**Scarcity Index—★★★★**

**Henry Mancini** (1924-1994)—One of the greatest film/TV composers of all time, Mancini has left a rich legacy that has touched all of our lives. Be it the cute and bouncy "Baby Elephant Walk," the jazzy theme to *The Pink Panther*, the suspenseful TV theme "Peter Gunn" or movie classics like *Moon River* (Oscar win) and more recently an Oscar win for the *Victor/Victoria* scores. He was always a willing signer of fan mail and in person requests, often taking the time to draw MQ's (Musical Quotes), which consist of bars of music from a famous song and then signing the song title and his name. The most famous and desirable MQS is from "Moon River," which sells at $150 when encountered. His signature alone is worth $40, and signed photographs sell at $75.
**Scarcity Index—★★**

**Fredric March** (1897-1975)—Although March starred in a number of good films in a long career, he is collected most for his performance in the title role of the first screen adaptation of *Dr. Jekyll and Mr. Hyde* in 1931. He won an Oscar, which makes him needed for Academy Award collectors. He was always a friendly signer and is not too hard to find—although getting tougher with each passing year. (He died of cancer in 1975.) His signature sells now for $50, with a photograph of him fetching $100. A photograph as "Jekyll" would bring much more than $100. Letters have sporadically hit the market in the $150-200 range, as have documents.
**Scarcity Index—★★★**

**Dean Martin** (1917-1996)—Dean Martin was a triple threat in the cinema. Not only could he do comedy and stage work as evidenced in his long career with Jerry Lewis, but he sang well too, and had many hit records. He produced movies and ran as a member of that influential group known as the "Rat Pack," with Frank Sinatra as their leader. He was a friendly signer, even after signing became a chore for him, due to health problems. During the last several years of his life, he employed secretaries to sign his fan mail, and dealers have often sold these as real (since it closely resembled a signature style of his from years earlier). Close examination of a real signature compared with a secretarial signature will show the subtle differences. So BE CAREFUL buying this one. Fortunately, you can buy one of his personal checks that were signed by him some twenty years earlier that have hit the market in the $100 plus range. Photographs are now in that same $100 range since his death. Signatures alone sell for $30. A few letters and other documents, such as recording deals, have sold in the $200 plus range. He is remembered by many collectors for his send up of James Bond's character in his own series of movies as "Matt Helm."
**Scarcity Index—Authentic ones ★★**

**Steve Martin** (1945-   )—Born in 1945 in Waco, Texas, Steve Martin first gained fame by his frequent skits on "Saturday Night Live." He then co-wrote his first film *The Jerk*, a critical and comic success followed by several less-praised films. However, in 1983, he hit big again with the film *All of Me* oppo-

site Lilly Tomlin. He has since broadened his acting in gentler roles, such as can be found in *Father of the Bride*, *Parenthood*, and *Leap of Faith*. He is a friendly signer, and has even answered some fan mail, keeping his signature affordable at $20, and signed photographs (funnier images sell better) at $50.

**Scarcity Index—★★**

**Lee Marvin** (1924-1987)—Marvin's career started as supporting-cast villains in a number of movies. He certainly paid his dues in these roles for 10 years plus before starring on his own in *The Wild One*, opposite none other than Marlon Brando. He was brilliant in *The Commanchero's* opposite John Wayne, as well as the classic *The Man Who Shot Liberty Valance*. He died in 1987, and was never an easy signature to obtain—which is why he sells for $200 plus as a signature, with photographs at $400. A few documents have sold in the $400 range, as well.

**Scarcity Index—★★★**

**Marx Brothers**—Several books have been written on the comic genius that is the Marx Brothers, and surely all readers know who they are. So we will deal mainly with their signing habits here. The original grouping of brothers were Groucho, Chico, Harpo, Zeppo, and Gummo. Zeppo (1901-1979) and Gummo (1897-1977) performed earlier in their pre-film career and Zeppo later managed them as agent (he managed many other stars as well). Primarily, when you think of the Marx Brothers you think of the trio of Groucho (1895-1977), Chico (1891-1961) and Harpo (1893-1961). The three signatures on one item is a scarce find—often they would sign separate album pages within an autograph book. If all three did sign one or separate pieces, they often only signed first names. Here it gets a little tricky: A full signature of Groucho Marx sells for $250, with full signatures of Chico selling for the same. Harpo is the rarest signature of the three with a full signature selling for $400. Therefore, a separate set of the three in full would run $900. But if the three signed only first names, the set would run $500, or approximately half their values across the board. If all three signed in full on the same piece of paper, they would sell for a premium of $1500. Signed photographs of the team are even rarer. A signed photograph of all three (first names only) would run $1500, with full names running as much as $2500. Documents are rare, with one signed by all three selling at auction a couple of years ago for $2000. Letters are rare on Chico and Harpo, but Groucho letters and documents have surfaced, averaging $400 each. Signed photographs of them individually would be $250, $400, and $600 for Groucho, Chico, and Harpo, respectively. Groucho Marx's checks have also hit the market at $200 each. Zeppo Marx's checks hit the market bringing $100 each. Gummo's signature for the completist who wants to own all of the Marx clan will run you $150.

**Scarcity Index—Groucho ★★ Chico ★★★**
**Harpo ★★★★ All Three Together ★★★★**

**Hattie McDaniel** (1895-1952)—One of the rarest signatures to obtain when collecting the cast from *Gone with the Wind*, McDaniel was the first black actress to win an Academy Award, for her portrayal of the "Mammy" in the classic film. She was Emmy-nominated for her TV series "Beulah," as well, but died far too young in 1952, further complicating efforts to obtain her autograph. America was a different and more segregated place in her day, which is why her autograph is rare today, selling for $500 plus. Documents and photographs are so scarce they can fetch $1000-1500 when encountered. Her contract from *Gone with the Wind* sold privately for $7500 last year.
Scarcity Index—★★★★★

**Butterfly McQueen** (1911-1995)—"Prissy" from *Gone with the Wind* will always be remembered for not knowing "nothing 'bout birthin' no babies." One of the last cast members to pass away, she died in 1995 in a tragic house fire from a faulty kerosene heater. She had signed at shows, through fan mail, and in person for years, as well as numerous photographs in character. A signature sells for $50, with in-character photographs selling for $125. A number of her personal checks were sold to collectors (she sold many herself), and these can currently be found at around $100.
Scarcity Index—★★

**Steve McQueen** (1930-1980)—For an actor who starred in his own action films for years as a superstar, McQueen certainly had an inauspicious beginning. His first film was a science fiction B movie called *The Blob*! He is more remembered, fortunately, for films like *Bullitt* and *The Magnificent Seven*. He died of cancer in 1980, and left his fans wanting more, and autograph collectors paying more! A signature sells for $200, with photographs fetching $400. A very few documents have sold in the $500 range as well. Be careful with his signature as his wife signed most of his fan mail.
Scarcity Index—★★★★

**Ethel Merman** (1909-1984)—Nothing on screen equaled her Broadway successes, such as in *Annie Get Your Gun* and her signature role in *Gypsy*. She played a great comic parody of herself in *It's a Mad, Mad, Mad, Mad World* in 1963, but not much of note after. She was a friendly signer in person and answered some fan mail late in life. Her signature sells for $40 currently, with signed photographs at $100. A few documents have sold in the $100-150 range at auction.
Scarcity Index—★★★

**Robert Mitchum** (1917-1997)—Mitchum seemed destined to play the heavy in role after role due to his large build, deep voice, and cocky expressions. In fact, he started as villains in some early *Hopalong Cassidy* films before signing with RKO in 1944, who gave him his biggest break by starring him in a couple of western films. He went on to play tough guys in film after film for many studios, turning in solid performances each time. In 1954, he starred opposite a young Marilyn Monroe in *River of No Return*. He has stayed with made-for-TV movies and mini-series ever since 1975, with critical raves for his performances in the *Winds of War* and *War and Remembrance*. He has signed some fan mail off and on, and was a friendly signer in person. His signature sells at $20, with a signed photograph at $50 (western and war images are best). Scarcity Index—★★

**Marilyn Monroe** (1926-1962)—More biographies have been written about her than any other star, and she is the most photographed woman in the world to this day. So we'll concentrate here on her signing habits. During her heyday, it was more difficult to get Monroe's signature than even the president of the United States! Then, she died suddenly in her prime, making herself a legend, as well as the most expensive entertainment figure for autograph collectors to collect. She used secretaries to sign her fan mail, so BE CAREFUL when buying a Monroe, and be sure you are dealing with a reputable dealer who has handled Monroe signatures before, and offers a Lifetime Guarantee of Authenticity. A fair number of her business and personal checks have made it to the market, and sell for around $3000 for checks signed by her but typed, and $4000 for checks she filled out entirely in her own hand. Handwritten letters sell for $5000 and up, depending on content, with signed photographs in the same range. Documents signed with her real name, Norma Jean Doherty, sell for as much as $7500. Memorable films include *Some Like it Hot*, *Niagara*, *The Prince and the Showgirl*, and *Gentlemen Prefer Blondes*.
Scarcity Index—★★★★

**Demi Moore** (1962-  )—Demi Moore has come a long way since she started on the soap opera, "General Hospital," to being the highest paid actress in Hollywood. In her movie *Striptease*, she was paid $12 million. She turned in great performances along the way in *Ghost* and *A Few Good Men*. She is a friendly signer, and would be friendlier if not for her overprotective actor/husband Bruce Willis, who, by stopping her signing on so many occasions, has kept her signature scarce and valuable at $200 on a photograph, and $75 as a signature. Perhaps he'll loosen up in the future. A document relating to her early "General Hospital" days sold recently for $400.
**Scarcity Index—★★★**

**Roger Moore** (1927-  )—Even if Moore never appeared in another film he would always be collected for playing James Bond 007 after Sean Connery, in a number of Bond films, starting with *Live and Let Die*. He lives in England and is getting tougher to get as a signature, which currently sells at $25, with a Bond signed photograph (What Else?) selling around $75. A few documents (none dealing with Bond movies) have sold in the $100 range. He would play Bond six more times, ending with *A View to a Kill* in 1985.
**Scarcity Index—★★**

**Frank Morgan** (1890-1949)—From the stage to the screen, Morgan played a wide range of character roles to much acclaim, but collectors only seem to care about one: the "Great and Magical Wizard of Oz" in the film classic from 1939. In fact, he played several roles in that film, including the Wizard, the floating projected head of the Wizard, the carriage driver in the Emerald City, the guard who answered the gate at the Emerald City, and "Professor Marvel" from the beginning scenes.
Photographs as the "Wizard" do not exist because Morgan died before the film achieved the success once it was released annually to TV in 1956. Regular, signed portraits sell for $600, with signatures selling for $400. Documents have hit the market in the $700 range.
**Scarcity Index—★★★★**

**Audie Murphy** (1924-1971)—A great western star, Murphy was also the most decorated soldier in America in WWII. He played himself in the movie *To Hell and Back* in 1955. Unexpectedly, Murphy died in a plane crash in 1971 at only 46 years of age. He was a friendly signer in person, but is uncommon due to his untimely death. A signature sells for $125, with signed photographs at $300. Documents have sold in the $300 range as well.

**Scarcity Index**—★★★

**Patricia Neal** (1926-  )—Born in 1926, Neal seemed to try matching her dramatic roles with a dramatic private life. Her breakout film role was in *The Fountainhead* in 1949, but nearly overshadowing her great critical reviews were stories of her sensational affair with her married co-star Gary Cooper. She suffered a nervous breakdown when they ended their affair. Next, she suffered through losing two children she had with actor Roald Dahl. (One was struck down by a car, and one died from measles.) She divorced him and then suffered a series of strokes, which she triumphantly worked through, and continued acting, although mainly in TV movies. She has been very gracious signing for fans by mail and in person. She is an Oscar winner, and is collected for that reason, but also collected on photographs from the sci-fi classic *The Day the Earth Stood Still*, which sells at $50. (Signatures at $20.)

**Scarcity Index**—★

**Pola Negri** (1894-1987)—One of film's first German inports, Pola Negri was one of silent film's greatest stars, but did not make the transition to talkies. She would do films in the talkie era in Europe, but never made it back in the United States again. She is a must for collectors of the silent era, however. Having died in 1987, she is fairly common, with her signature selling in the $30-40 range, and signed photographs at $100.

**Scarcity Index**—★★★

**Paul Newman** (1925-   )—Born in 1925, Newman is the Oscar-winning legend of such film classics as *Butch Cassidy and the Sundance Kid*, *The Sting*, and *The Hustler*. He is friendly with fans and willing to talk and shake hands, but he does not like to sign autographs. What further messes up the market is the fact that he employs secretaries to sign his mail, and many dealers who do not know better (or do not care) sell them. An authentic signature sells easily for $125, with authentic photographs selling for $300. Letters and documents are scarcer, although a number (approx. 200) of personal checks have hit the market that currently sell for $200 each.

**Scarcity Index—★★★**

**Jack Nicholson** (1937-   )—Born in 1937, Jack may seem intimidating from his performances in *One Flew Over the Cukoo's Nest* and in the Stephen King classic *The Shining*. But he is an accommodating signer in person, and quite friendly. His signature sells for around $30, with the more collectible signed photographic images (*The Shining* and as the "Joker" from Batman) selling at  $80. A few documents have sold in the $200 range. Other memorable films include *A Few Good Men*, *Chinatown*, and *Terms of Endearment*.

**Scarcity Index—★★**

**Donald O'Connor** (1925-   )—O'Connor never seemed to be given the roles that would make him a superstar, but he could do drama, and comedy, and could sing and dance with equal ease. He will always be remembered (and collected) for playing opposite Gene Kelly in the classic *Singing in the Rain*. Signed photographs from the classic movie sell for $50, with his autograph selling at $20. He has signed some fan mail in the past, and has always been a friendly signer when approached in person.

**Scarcity Index—★**

**Laurence Olivier** (1907-1989)—Many fans and actors alike feel that Olivier was the greatest actor to grace the screen, certainly a great Shakespearean actor, and considered great enough to be knighted by the Queen as "Sir" Laurence Olivier. The roles for which he is collected, beyond being an Oscar winner, are varied—as "Von Helsing" on Broadway and film versions of *Dracula* and in *Pride and Prejudice* as "Mr. Darcy." He starred in *Rebecca*, *Wuthering Heights*, *Henry V*, and *Hamlet*. Many collectors also want him for directing and co-starring with Marilyn Monroe in *The Prince and the Showgirl*, which he starred in on Broadway opposite his wife, Vivien Leigh. In 1987, on his 80th birthday he announced his retirement in all but radio roles. (He died in 1989.) During his later years, he signed much of his fan mail and his signature takes on two forms. Sometimes he signed the full "Laurence Olivier" and other times he signed "L'Olivier." A full signature is worth around $50 with a signed photograph at $100 and up depending on the image. "L'Olivier" signatures are worth approximately 25 percent less on either. Letters and documents have hit the market in the $150 range.

**Scarcity Index—★★**

**Gregory Peck** (1916-1996)—Peck was a good, solid actor who had flashes of brilliance, such as in *To Kill a Mockingbird*, the movie version of Harper Lee's Pulitzer Prize-winning novel, or opposite Audrey Hepburn in *Roman Holiday*. He was always a gracious signer, including years of signing fan mail, keeping his signature at $25, and photographs at around $60. A few documents and letters have sold in the $150 range. He is collected by Oscar-winner collectors for having won for his portrayal in *To Kill a Mockingbird*.

**Scarcity Index—★★**

**Anthony Perkins** (1932-1992)—Although he enjoyed a long and varied career in the cinema, "Tony" Perkins will always be remembered for starring in the Hitchcock classic *Psycho* in 1960. In fact, he starred in the sequel *Psycho II*, and both starred and directed *Psycho III*. (He died of AIDS in 1992.) He was  always a friendly signer in person and in the last couple of years of his life, he signed *Psycho* photographs by mail for some fans. A signed portrait is a hard sell for dealers today at $50, but a *Psycho* shot of Perkins sells for $200 and up, more if signed by his famous co-star, Janet Leigh (herself a gracious signer). A signature alone sells for $65.

**Scarcity Index—★★★**

**River Phoenix** (1971-1993)—It remains to be seen if River's body of work would have made him collectible, for it was his tragic death on the sidewalk in front of actor Johnny Depp's club "The Viper Room" that made him a collectible name due to its rarity. A signature sells now for $200, with signed photographs selling at $400, as have a couple of documents. Memorable film roles include *Stand By Me, Running on Empty*, and as a young "Indiana Jones" in *Indiana Jones and the Last Crusade*. He was set to film the movie *Interview with a Vampire* when he died, thus giving the role to Tom Cruise.

**Scarcity Index—★★★★**

**Mary Pickford** (1893-1979)—America's sweetheart during the silent era, also called "the Girl with the Curls," Mary Pickford was America's first film star. In the incredible early days of film (1914) she was already earning $1000 a week. By 1915, only one year later, it was $2000 per week. The next year she went to $4000 per week and a year later, $10,000 per week! Details of any new salary or other business arrangements with America's Sweetheart was always front page news. She said in her memoirs that whenever the new rage, Charlie Chaplin, got a wage increase, she pushed to get a bigger one. In 1920, she married actor Douglas Fairbanks Sr., and along with Chaplin and director D.W. Griffith, they formed United Artists. Originally, the foursome formed their company amid rumors that the studios, who felt their stars' salaries were getting too high, were going to put a ceiling on them. She was one of the first women to win an Oscar for her first talkie performance in *Coquette* in 1929. Her next three movie choices were bad, and rather than rebuild her career she decided to retire in 1935. In her retirement years, she frequently answered her fan mail which was quite large. Her signature is worth $60 currently, with signed photographs selling for $150. Typed letters have surfaced in that same range, mostly dealing with charity work she did in the 1950s and 1960s.
Scarcity Index—★★★

**Brad Pitt** (1963-    )—*People* magazine waited three years after naming Sean Connery as their "Sexiest Man Alive," because they said no one was worthy. Then they bestowed the title again to young superstar Brad Pitt. After critical acclaim in *A River Runs Through It, Cool World*, and *Thelma and Louise*, Pitt's popularity soared. He turned in another great performance in *Interview with a Vampire* opposite Tom Cruise, and then again in *Legends of the Fall*. There appears to be no end in sight for this rising star. His most collectible images are from *Interview* and *Legends of the Fall*. These photographs sell for $75, with a signature selling for $35. Documents and letters have yet to hit the market. His fan mail is currently answered by secretaries who sign with a long legible signature that does not resemble his. Stay tuned to this man's exciting career; we think he will only go up in value and demand.
Scarcity Index—★★

**Tyrone Power** (1913-1958)—A capable actor in films for over twenty years (1937-1957), and a matinee idol because of his good looks, Power died of a heart attack while filming a scene with George Sanders in 1958. He will probably best be remembered for the role of bullfighter in *Blood and Sand,* and for his performance in *The Razor's Edge.* Having died so long ago, his signature is uncommon and sells for $150, with photographs at around $350. A few documents have hit the market in the $300 range, but are more uncommon. Other memorable roles include *The Sun Also Rises* and *Rawhide.* **Scarcity Index—★★★**

**Vincent Price** (1911-1993)—One of the kings of horror, Price starred in many horror classics (some in 3-D) like *House of Wax, Mad Magician*, and *The Fly*. He was an amateur artist (of some talent) who often did a self caricature for fans in various sizes. These sell today for $150 for a smaller 3" x 5" size and up. Signed photographs sell for around $100, with signatures worth $45. A few letters and documents have sold for $200 and up, and quite a few checks hit the market (approx. 400) that sell for around $100, signed "Vincent L. Price Jr." (his full legal name). **Scarcity Index —★★    Sketches ★★★**

**George Raft** (1903-1980)—As a gangster in films, Raft was one of the best. *Scarface* in 1932 made him famous. Bear in mind, it was based on the life of Al Capone, who was still alive at the time, and he allegedly threatened Raft's life if he played him in a film. He was so identified for the rest of his career as this kind of character that he even played a gang boss in a small role in the Marilyn Monroe film, *Some Like it Hot*, in 1959. He died penniless in 1980. His signature runs $60, with a signed photograph at $150. **Scarcity Index—★★★**

**Claude Rains** (1889-1967)—Collectors have two very good reasons to collect Claude Rains. Well, actually three, if you count because he was a great actor. But, the other two are *Casablanca* and *The Invisible Man.* He was also in the *Wolf Man* as the wolf's father, as well as the lead in *The Phantom of the Opera.* He died in 1967, however, and is an uncommon autograph to find, running $150 for a signature, and $250 on a signed photograph. As the "Invisible Man," a signed photograph would fetch more. One document has sold in the last several years for $400. **Scarcity Index—★★★★**

**Sally Rand** (1903-1979)—The Queen of the fan dancers, sexy Sally Rand starred in a few films in the twenties and thirties at the height of her dancing popularity. Sexy photographs signed by her can be had at $100, with her signature alone selling for $50. She died in 1979, having signed much fan mail in her retirement years.
**Scarcity Index—★★★**

**Basil Rathbone** (1892-1967)—Many actors played "Sherlock Holmes" and will be collected for having done so. But Rathbone, to most people, was the definitive Sherlock Holmes and starred in the most movies as the famous detective. For horror collectors, he starred in *Son of Frankenstein* in 1939 opposite Lugosi and Karloff. He swashbuckled with Tyrone Power in the classic *Mark of Zorro*, too. Since he died in 1967, and is an uncommon signature, he sells for $250, with signed photographs at $400, although, as Holmes, one would pay $500 and up. A couple of documents have hit the market in the $500 range, and a few letters have sold around $700 in which he discussed playing Sherlock Holmes.
**Scarcity Index—★★★★**

**Robert Redford** (1937-   )—From starring opposite Paul Newman in classics like *The Sting* and *Butch Cassidy and the Sundance Kid*, to giving Demi Moore an *Indecent Proposal*, Redford is as big a star today as twenty years ago. He owns his own production company, Sundance Films, that gives small filmmakers breaks into the business. He employs secretaries to sign his mail. Although examination of his authentic signature next to the secretaries show obvious differences, sadly, this hasn't stopped neophyte dealers from selling them, so BE CAREFUL. An authentic signature is worth $75, and photographs around $200. A number of his signed personal checks have been on the market that currently sell for $200.
**Scarcity Index—★★★**

**George Reeves** (1914-1959)—The original TV "Superman" was a huge star in his day, on his way to movie stardom, (he was even in *Gone with the Wind*) and then came "Superman." Sure, it was a steady paycheck, but it hopelessly typecast him. He was very depressed after it ended his ability to find other roles, so much so that he killed himself in his home while hosting a small party one night. Although many were at the party, no one witnessed the grisly scene upstairs in his bedroom. Many believe he was murdered, but enough evidence did not exist for the police to pursue this line. Either way, a rare signature was born when somebody proved that night that he really wasn't faster than a speeding bullet. Collectors from *Gone with the Wind* to "Superman" have clamored for the few signatures that show up on the market each year. His *Gone with the Wind* contract sold recently for $6000, but few other letters or documents have hit the market. His signature sells for $800 plus, with a signed portrait selling for $1200. Many times he signed photographs of himself as Superman signing "Best Wishes, Superman" and did not add his real name, since he felt that it would ruin the illusion for a child. These are still collectible, but in the same range as a portrait. HOWEVER, a signed photograph as Superman with his real name is worth more than $1500. Watch out for forgeries and secretarial signatures who answered the huge amount of fan mail he recieved in the 1950s. An interesting "Super" story is that on a personal appearance tour in which he naturally wore his famous costume, a kid who had stolen Daddy's gun from home attempted to shoot Reeves to prove to friends that bullets would truly bounce off the "superhero." Reeves refused to ever again wear the suit in public.
Scarcity Index—★★★★

**Debbie Reynolds** (1932-    )—Charming and cute, Reynolds has had a long career, but will always be remembered for her starring role opposite Gene Kelly in the film classic *Singing in the Rain*. She would play mostly lighthearted musicals from that film on. She retired in 1974 until 1996, when after a 22-year absence, she starred in *Mother* opposite Albert Brooks, and won an Oscar nomination for her performance in it. She owns her own memorabilia museum, housed in her own hotel in Las Vegas, where she still performs in small cabaret shows. She is a friendly signer in person, and has signed fan mail in the past, as well. A signature is worth $15, with signed photographs from *Singing in the Rain* selling at $50. Letters have sold at $50 as well.
Scarcity Index—★

**Julia Roberts** (1967-    )—Beautiful actress Julia Roberts of *Pretty Woman* fame has always been hesitant to sign for fans, and does not sign fan mail either, thus keeping the price of her signature rather high, currently at $50 for a signature, and $125 on a photograph. A couple of bank documents have sold around $200, but she is still quite young, and who knows what the future holds? Memorable films so far include *Hook, The Pelican Brief,* and *I Love Trouble.*
**Scarcity Index—★★★**

**Edward G. Robinson** (1893-1973)—Along with Cagney and Raft, Robinson found his acting niche as a gangster on film. He once said that the middle initial "G" in his name stood for "gangsters." In 1930, *Little Caeser* launched his fame in that direction, which he solidified for the next twenty years. He died in 1973, sadly, just days before he was to be awarded a special Oscar for Lifetime Achievement in Film. His signature is worth $60, with a photograph at $200 or more. Documents are scarce, except for checks, of which quite a few were found—many had been thrown away and cut in half—these sell in the $75 range. Other memorable films include *Key Largo* and *The Ten Commandments.*
**Scarcity Index—★★★**

**Ginger Rogers** (1911-1995)—The other half of the world famous Astaire and Rogers dance team was also an accomplished actress with many credits to her career. She died in 1995 after years of being an obliging signer in person and of her fan mail. She even did a private signing of approximately 400 photographs the year she died, for a small autograph dealer who markets them at $200 each. Her signature is worth $50, and documents sell around $200 like the photographs. Film highlights include *Swing Time, The Gay Divorcee,* and *Follow the Fleet.*
**Scarcity Index—★★**

**Roy Rogers** (1912-  )—Of all the western stars, no one has been more loved than Roy and his famous horse Trigger (now stuffed and on display in Roy's museum), or his talented cowgirl wife, Dale. In fact, he and his wife have only stopped signing for fans in the last two years, and prices are already starting to rise.  For years they were very gracious signers at western events and through the mail for fans, but health concerns have stopped that now. A Roy Rogers signature is $30 currently, with a photograph selling at $60. A signed card by both Dale and Roy sells at $50, with a joint signed photograph at $100. Roy often signed Trigger's name to photographs, picturing them both, and also signed his famous quote "Happy Trails" on photographs, as well.

**Scarcity Index—★★**

**Will Rogers** (1879-1935)—If Mary Pickford was America's sweetheart, than surely Will Rogers was America's humorist. He was actually only in a few movies, establishing his fame instead on stage and radio. His wit and homespun take on current affairs and politics have left us with a legacy of truisms. He was taken far too soon from us in a tragic plane crash, despite the fact that a world famous aviator was at the controls, Wiley Post, who also died in the crash. The crash happened in 1935, which has made his signature quite rare, selling for $400, with photographs at  $800. Documents and letters are even rarer and more valuable.

**Scarcity Index—★★★★**

**Mickey Rooney** (1920-   )—Like most child stars, it was inevitable that Rooney could not stay on top forever, but it looked for awhile as if he might.  He is most famous for a series of "Andy Hardy" films he did with famous co-star Judy Garland. He is still very active today, and signs willingly, which has kept his signature at $15, and photographs at $30. Some documents in the $100 range have hit the market, as have some letters with normal content. He also did a signing for a private autograph firm recently that markets his signed photographs at $30.
**Scarcity Index—★**

**Rosalind Russell** (1911-1976)—Russell had an incredible ability to perform light comedy bits, although none as remembered as her award-winning performance as "Auntie Mame." She was an accomplished stage and musical actress, as well. She died in 1976. Her signature sells for $60, with signed photographs at $125. A small number of her personal checks have hit the market in the $75 range, with some letters having sold in the same range. Other film credits include *No Time for Comedy* and *A Woman of Distinction*.
**Scarcity Index—★★**

**Meg Ryan** (1961-   )—The adorable blonde actress has already made a name for herself in a series of hit movies like *When Harry Met Sally*, *Top Gun*, and *Sleepless in Seattle*. She is a tough signer in person, however, and does not, as yet, sign fan mail—keeping her signature pricey at $40, with signed photographs at $75.
**Scarcity Index—★★★**

**Charles M. Schulz** (1922-    )—One of, if not the most successful cartoonists of all times, the creator of "Peanuts" (Charlie Brown, Snoopy and the gang) has been a syndicated feature cartoon in more newspapers around the world than any other cartoonist in history. Due to age, Mr. Schultz has stopped signing and sketching for fans, but did so for many years. He only rarely signed his full name, opting usually to sign simply "Schulz." A small headshot sketch of Snoopy or any Peanuts member signed sells for around $275, with a signature alone valued at $50. The larger and more detailed the artwork or sketch, the more value it has.

**Scarcity Index—★★★**

**Randolph Scott** (1903-1987)—Considered one of the all time great western film actors, Scott is a must for western collectors. He starred in *Jesse James*, *The Gunfighters*, and *The Last Roundup* to name a few. He died in 1987, one of the last of the great western stars. He was a friendly signer but rarely answered fan mail, so is more uncommon than most stars that lived as long. A signature sells for $50, and $125 for a signed photograph. Documents are scarcer, with a few letters having sold in the $100 range.

**Scarcity Index—★★★**

**Steven Seagal** (1952-    )—With his trademark ponytail and huge frame, no other action/martial arts star resembles Seagal. He can be quite charming on screen as proven in *Under Siege*, which was the first film to seek a wider audience than his earlier fight films. He married actress Kelly LeBrock, and is a friendly signer in person. However, BEWARE, as many secretarial-signed photographs that are sent in the mail have been sold by unknowledgeable dealers.

**Scarcity Index—★★**

**Tom Selleck** (1945-    )—Although he has had mild success in films he is collected mainly for his starring role in the TV series "Magnum PI." He has signed some fan mail, and is a friendly signer in person, keeping his signature at $20. A "Magnum PI"-signed photograph is worth $50. He is starring in a new sitcom on TV after testing his popularity in a recurring role on TV's "Friends," as Courtney Cox's older lover.

**Scarcity Index—★★**

**Peter Sellers** (1925-1980)—Although turning in great performances in films like *Being There*, Sellers will always be remembered and collected as "Inspector Clouseau" in the hilarious *Pink Panther* films. He died of a heart attack in 1980, leaving collectors clamoring for an uncommon signature valued at $100, with photographs at $200. *Pink Panther* shots sell for up to $300. A few documents have sold for $200 and up as well. Sellers never signed fan mail, and was a hesitant signer in person.

**Scarcity Index—★★★**

**Norma Shearer** (1904-1983)—Beautiful, glamorous, and intensely popular with her fans, Shearer was on top of the box office in the early 1930s, and only slipped in popularity due to her own desire to work less. She accepted the role of "Scarlet" in *Gone with the Wind,* and then turned it down because her fans (through her fan clubs) disapproved of her playing the part! She died in 1983, and although she signed in her heyday, she rarely signed in old age, keeping her price at $100 for a signature, and $300 on a photograph. Documents and letters are scarcer. Memorable film roles include *Divorcee* (Oscar win), *Romeo and Juliette,* and *Private Lives.*
**Scarcity Index—★★★★**

**Phil Silvers** (1912-1985)—Although he appeared in many movies, Phil Silvers will always be remembered as "Sgt. Ernie Bilko" on "The Phil Silvers Show," which ran on TV from 1955-1958. He died in 1985, and although he often signed in person, he rarely answered fan mail, making his signature uncommon and worth $40, with "Sgt. Bilko" signed photographs valued at $150. A few letters have sold in the $200 range.
**Scarcity Index—★★★**

**Frank Sinatra** (1917-   )—"The Chairman of the Board" has led a charmed life full of successes in film, stage, and as a great singer. He is the honorary founder of the "Rat Pack," of which he and Joey Bishop are the only living members. Sinatra has stopped signing in the past couple of years because he has begun shaking and cannot see as well. He has always signed for fans if approached with respect, but employed only secretaries to sign his name on fan mail. He turned down a reported $5 million to sign for a major shopping channel, and it appears this legend's signature will only get more valuable as time goes on. His signature currently sells for $150, with photographs selling for $300 plus, and the few documents that have surfaced selling for $500 and up. Memorable films include *From Here to Eternity*, *Ship Ahoy*, and *None but the Brave*.

Scarcity Index—★★★

**Red Skelton** (1911-1997)—Comedian Red Skelton starred in many films as well as having his own TV series. During his retirement years, he continued with his passion as a painter, specifically of clowns. (He started in the business as a clown.) His paintings sell in the thousands of dollars today. As the value of his signed paintings skyrocketed, he stopped signing, and passed away in 1997 at 86. Fortunately, he was such a gracious signer for fans for so many years that he is an easy autograph to obtain, selling for $45, and $125 on a photograph. A number of personal checks signed "Richard Red Skelton" sell in the $100 range.

Scarcity Index—★★

**Barbara Stanwyck** (1907-1990)—Although she had starred in dozens of movies opposite everyone from Elvis Presley to William Holden, it is in later years as the tough-as-nails mother and household head of the clan on the TV show "The Big Valley" that she is collected for today. She died in 1990 and had won a special Lifetime Achievement Oscar in 1982. She was a friendly signer and signed fan mail off and on in later years. Her signature sells for $35, with a photograph at $100. Documents and letters have sold in the same $100 range. Prior to success on TV, her film roles included *Double Indemnity*; *East Side, West Side*; and *Roustabout*.
**Scarcity Index—★★**

**James Stewart** (1908-1997)—Without a doubt, as the lovable star of over 100 motion pictures—many classics—including *Vertigo*, *It's a Wonderful Life*, and *Harvey*, Jimmy Stewart was as American as apple pie. He served in the air force as a pilot and rose to the rank of colonel. He spent years in retirement answering fan mail, but after his wife's death in 1994, he had a stroke himself, from which he never fully recovered, passing away in 1997. His mail was answered the last few years of his life using an autopen to sign photographs. He has signed "Jimmy" and "James Stewart" over the years (which are equal in value). Due to his prodigious signing, he is reasonable at $40 as a signature, and $125 as a signed photograph. Approximately 400 personal checks have hit the market, and currently sell in the $150-200 range. (Other documents and letters sell for more.) Stewart also published a book of poetry which you will find signed from time to time. His own personal favorite among the 100 plus movies he performed in was the 1950 classic *Harvey*, which he loved so much that he performed it often on Broadway for years. For a period of time, from the late 1970s to the late 1980s, he drew sketches of the imaginary rabbit from the film *Harvey* and signed them. The sketches range in size from 3" x 5" (that currently sell for $350) to larger sketches that sell for more. These are classic pieces of art to own, and time is running out to buy one at a reasonable rate.
**Scarcity Index—★     Sketches ★★**

**Sharon Stone** (1958-   )—Her first five films did not leave a ripple in the waters of fame for Stone. *Total Recall* got her noticed a bit more, but it would be as the manipulative bi-sexual murder suspect in *Basic Instinct* that would set her fame and begin a series of better movie roles. She has since sunk her acting teeth into such films as *The Specialist*, *Diabolique*, and *The Quick and the Dead*. She does not sign fan mail, but is a friendly signer when approached. Her signature currently sells at $30, with $50 on sexy photographs. (The most classic of which is legs crossed in the chair smoking the cigarette while being interrogated in *Basic Instinct*.) A few signed personal checks that she signs "S.Stone" have sold at $100 each, as well as a few other documents.
**Scarcity Index—★★**

**Barbra Streisand** (1942-   )—The great vocal talents of Streisand are unmatched, but she is a great actress on stage or screen as well. In her own way she must appreciate her fans, because she pays out of her own pocket to maintain three different addresses that handle fan mail—unfortunately, all signed by her secretaries. Although she tries to handle fan mail, she is one of the toughest signers in person, often only signing "Barbra" or more often, not at all. She even has stopped other celebrities from signing when approached near her! This is why authentic material is scarce, with signed photographs selling for $400, and a signature at $200. A few documents and checks have sold in the $600-700 range. BE CAREFUL, because many dealers still sell the secretarial signed photographs gotten through the mail. The differences are subtle but consistent when looking at an authentic "Barbra" versus her secretaries' signatures. Memorable films include *What's Up Doc?*, *Hello Dolly*, and *The Way We Were*.
**Scarcity Index—★★★**

**Gloria Swanson** (1899-1983)—Swanson and Pickford are the most famous silent film stars to this day. She won an Oscar in the Oscar's first year, 1928. She retired in 1950, and collectors need her not only as an Oscar winner, but for the classic film *Sunset Blvd.*, where she utters the immortal screen dialogue, "I'm ready for my closeup, Mr. Demille." She often signed fan mail during her retirement years. Her signature is valued today at $50, with photographs at $150. *Sunset Blvd.* photographs sell for more.
**Scarcity Index—★★**

**Lyle Talbot** (1902-1996)—Never breaking out of the B movie role, Talbot is still collected by sci-fi collectors for having starred in director Ed Wood's infamous *Planet Nine from Outerspace* and *Glen or Glinda.* He also starred in many western films as well as playing "Commissioner Gordon" in the early "Batman" serials of the forties, and villain "Lex Luther" in the first *Superman* film. He had done conventions for years, signing for fans until passing away a year ago. He also had signed fan mail for years prior to his death. A signature sells for $20, with signed photographs in one of the aforementioned roles selling for $50 plus.
**Scarcity Index—★★**

**Elizabeth Taylor** (1932-  )—What Brando is to high-priced living actors who rarely sign, Taylor is to actresses. She is very tough to get to and rarely signs, making her signature worth $200 for this Oscar-winning actress, and $500 on a photograph. A few documents have sold in the $700-plus range, unlike Brando, who doesn't answer fan mail or use secretaries to sign mail. Unfortunately, Liz uses secretaries to sign her mail, which some unknowledgeable dealers sell as real. BE CAREFUL. Born in 1932, La Liz has had many memorable film roles such as in *Cat on a Hot Tin Roof* and *Who's Afraid of Virginia Woolf?* She currently has her own line of prestige perfumes. Having recently been diagnosed with a brain tumor, she is recovering after what doctors have termed a successful surgery. Our best wishes are with you, Liz. Other memorable roles include *National Velvet* and *The Flintstones.*
**Scarcity Index—★★★★**

**Shirley Temple** (1928-   )—Certainly Temple is the King and Queen of all child stars. She singlehandedly kept her studio in black ink in good times and bad. She danced with Buddy Ebsen, Bill Bojangles Robinson, and sang and acted her way into America's heart.  As a teen in movies she starred opposite John Agar (whom she married and later divorced) and legends like Claudette Colbert and David Niven. She retired around 1957, and in 1969, President Nixon appointed her as a representative to the United Nations. In 1974, she became Ambassador to Ghana and married again. She signs for fans, but ever since her marriage over 20 years ago, she signs "Shirley Temple Black," which is a $20 signature, and a $50 photograph. Her teen years (1940s and 1950s) signature goes for $150, with a photograph easily topping $350. Her childhood years are the best to collect, with a photograph hitting $750, and signatures at $350. Letters written as a child have hit the market in the $400-plus range, depending on content, but documents from this time period are rare. She is one of few performers who have spawned collectibles in their image that have also risen in value. Have you priced an original Shirley Temple doll lately? Be careful of modern, signed photographs that are not signed "Black." Trust me, they were, but the name "Black" has been chemically erased to try to enhance the value of the piece to an unsuspecting collector.

**Scarcity Index—As a child  ★★★★ As a teen  ★★★**
**As Shirley Temple Black★**

**Three Stooges** —We could fill a book on this one comedy team that has brought so much laughter into generations of lives, but we will leave that for capable biographers and, instead, concentrate on their autographic history. Indeed, who are the Three Stooges? They changed over the years. The most famous team of three consisted of Moe Howard with brother Curly Howard and their friend Larry Fine. A signed page by all three is so scarce that even if only first names were signed (which was typical for them to do), it will cost as much as $1500. They also often signed variations on their names and nicknames such as Moe "Bangs" Howard, (referring to his straight black hairstyle); Larry "Fuzzy" Fine, (also a reference to his hairstyle); and Jerome "Curly" Howard (who was bald). When the rarest autograph in the set—the original Curly died in 1952—the act brought in another brother, Shemp Howard, who had performed back in the vaudeville days with them. He left the group and they tried to fill the popular shoes of brother Curly by bringing in "Curly Joe" Derita, and after Derita, "Curly Joe" Besser. All of these comedians are dead today, with Derita dying last and signing the most. Letters of Moe, Larry, and Curly Joe have hit the market and sold, depending on content, in the $200-400 range. Checks have surfaced of Curly Joe Derita at around $80 each, as have checks of Moe Howard and Shemp Howard at around $450 each. Signatures separately sell for around $200, $150, and $450 for Moe, Larry, and Curly Howard. Shemp's signature sells for around $150 with Joe Besser's at around $50, as does Derita's. A signed photograph of the original three brought $2500 at auction.

**Scarcity Index — w/Curly Howard ★★★★★**

**Franchot Tone** (1905-1969)—Leading male star of the 1930s who starred opposite his actress/wife, Joan Crawford, several times, as well as the other leading actresses of the day, such as Bette Davis and Katherine Hepburn, to name but a few. He was a good, solid performer whose signature would be a welcome addition to any Golden Age of Hollywood collection. He died of cancer in 1969 while still performing. His signature is uncommon and brings $30, with a photograph at $100. Documents are scarce, but a few letters in the $150 range have surfaced. Memorable film roles include *Bombshell*, *I Love Trouble*, and *Here Comes the Groom*.

**Scarcity Index—★★★**

**Spencer Tracy** (1900-1967)—Most critics agree that Tracy was one of the greatest actors to ever hit the silver screen. His ex-lover, Katherine Hepburn, has said the same thing in books and to the press for years. He was a solid actor in the early part of his career, but unlike many whose careers dipped in popularity with age, Tracy's popularity entering old age seemed only to climb. A must for Oscar-winner collections, he won both for *Captains Courageous*, and *Boy's Town*, giving him back-to-back Oscar wins (the only actor to so until Tom Hanks won back to back Oscars in 1994 and 1995). Tracy died shortly after filming the classic *Guess Who's Coming to Dinner*, starring Hepburn. He was always a tough signature and did not answer fan mail, so his signature has continued to rise in value, and will most likely continue to rise in the future. Currently, it sells for $150, with a photograph at $350. Documents are scarcer, as are letters, and would sell for more.

**Scarcity Index—★★★★**

**John Travolta** (1954-    )—John Travolta's career has had many lives and incarnations, starting as "Vinnie Barbarino" on the TV series "Welcome Back Kotter." Today, there is no end in sight for this leading male actor. He was nominated recently for *Get Shorty* and *Pulp Fiction*. He uses secretaries to sign his fan mail, so be sure you are buying an authentic Travolta! He is a friendly signer in person, with a signature selling for $35, and a signed photograph worth $75. *Pulp Fiction*, *Saturday Night Fever*, and "Welcome Back Kotter" are the most collectible images.

**Scarcity Index—★★**

**Claire Trevor** (1909-    )—Born in 1909, Trevor was first noticed in her Oscar-winning performance opposite Edward G. Robinson in the film classic *Key Largo*. She went on to star in dozens of other films before landing opposite John Wayne in the classic *Stagecoach*. She also had a role in *The Babe Ruth Story*. She signed some fan mail but has not been heard of in many years. Her signature sells for $30, with signed photographs at $75.
**Scarcity Index—★★★**

**Sophie Tucker** (1884-1966)—The Russian-born vaudeville singer was billed as the last of the "red hot mamas," and her unique and sometimes bawdy style has been often imitated and admired by singers like Bette Midler. Signatures sell in the $50 range, with signed photographs and letters selling at $100.
**Scarcity Index—★★★**

**Lana Turner** (1920-1995)—Lana Turner had a long career for a film star (over 40 years). Zeppo Marx originally signed her to his agency, and she started in bit parts in 1937. Her most memorable performance came in the 1946 classic *The Postman Always Rings Twice*. She was doing bit parts on TV the last few years of her life—and signed a lot of her fan mail during that time. A signature now sells for $40, with a photograph selling at $100. Some letters have surfaced at around $100, as well.
**Scarcity Index—★★**

**Rudolph Valentino** (1895-1926)—It is not clear today if Valentino's silent film work would hold scrutiny as great acting, or if he is more remembered for dying so young, causing a nation of female fans to grieve. (In 1926, he died of a perforated ulcer). His signature is exceedingly rare today. Having been a star as popular as Marilyn or Elvis, he could barely stop to sign for fear of a mob. Then suddenly, at the height of his fame, and without warning, he was dead—over 70 years ago. His signature sells for $800, with photographs in the $1500-1800 range. Documents are rare, as are letters, and would undoubtably sell for more.

Scarcity Index—★★★★★

**Vivian Vance** (1913-1979)—The straight "man" to Lucille Ball through two TV series as "Ethel Mertz" and later, "Vivian," will always make this character actress' signature collectible. She is a scarce signature, having died of cancer in 1979 and having not signed fan mail in her retirement years. Her signature sells for $200, with signed photographs from "I Love Lucy" selling for $500. Documents are scarcer and sell for around $300, unless associated to the "Lucy" series, which would be more valuable.

Scarcity Index—★★★★

**Mamie Van Doren** (1931-   )—A platinum bombshell, the critics referred to her as the "poor man's Lana Turner." She starred in a series of "sexploitation" films such as *High School Confidential* and *Girls School*. One of the original breed of "sex kittens," she dropped from acting sight around 1960 when that genre of films started to wane in popularity. But she stayed in the headlines due to a jet-setting lifestyle that would have made Hugh Hefner proud. She re-emerged some years ago and began appearing at B-movie conventions, signing for fans and signing fan mail. Racy photographs signed sell at $40, with her signature selling at $20.

Scarcity Index—★

**Jon Voight** (1938-   )—Voight's breakout role hit early in his career in 1969 with *Midnight Cowboy*, although he is also well remembered for the 1972 film *Deliverance*. He never quite attained the same status in later films, although he put in a star turn in Tom Cruise's film *Mission Impossible* as "Mr. Phelps," the character originally played on the TV series by Peter Graves. Voight is a fairly friendly signer when approached, and has sporadically signed fan mail in the past. Signatures sell at $20, with signed photographs at $50.
**Scarcity Index—★★**

**John Wayne** (1907-1979)—The "Duke" is as American as apple pie and loved the world over. His list of films, both western and non-western, cover an impressive 25 years, including the John Ford classics. Born as Marion Morrison in 1907, he was first given bit parts in a 1929 movie because he was a set decorator and friends with the director. Late in an already impressive career (1969), he won an Oscar for *True Grit*, which would become his favorite picture. (He once said it was his favorite simply because of the good reviews and the Oscar win.) Wayne used an autopen to sign many of his photographs and fan mail requests, as well as several secretaries. There are several ways to look for a real "Wayne," such as the peculiar way he doubled back around the "o" in John. There are many bad Waynes on the market, and one must be especially careful when buying a signed photograph of him. Early in his career, he was a very unwilling signer—and material signed in the 1940s and 1950s is very rare. Letters have hit the market in the $700 range, as have photographs, with his signature alone selling at $400. Documents (from the end of his career, the 1970s) that have hit the market have sold for $900, although vintage material again brings higher prices, such as a movie contract that sold last year for $2500 for a movie he did in 1948. Memorable films include *Stagecoach*, *Ft. Apache*, *She Wore a Yellow Ribbon*, and *Rio Grande*.
**Scarcity Index—★★★**

**Jack Webb** (1920-1982)—The straight-laced "Joe Friday" from "Dragnet" started on radio and was a smash on TV as well. Jack Webb, by all accounts, was Joe Friday and a friendly signer for fans. However, he died of cancer in 1982, having rarely signed fan mail. Therefore, he is an uncommon signature today, selling for $50, with signed "Dragnet" photographs selling at $150. A few documents have sold in the same $150 range.
Scarcity Index—★★★

**Johnny Weissmuller** (1904-1979)—Of all of the actors who played "Tarzan," Weissmuller is best remembered because of the athletic prowess he brought to the role: He was a former Olympic swimmer, and he played Tarzan the longest. It began at MGM in 1932 for him with *Tarzan the Ape Man*. Maureen O'Sullivan would play Jane opposite him in the films that would eventually number six. He did two more (without Jane) and then got a new Jane in actress Brenda Joyce, with whom he would do more as Tarzan. He tried to expand on this theme in a series called *Jungle Jim*, and would make ten of these films. He retired thereafter in 1955, and died in 1979. His signature is very collectible today and sells in the $150 range, with signed portraits selling for $175, and photographs as "Tarzan" bringing $250 and up.
Scarcity Index—★★★

**Orson Welles** (1915-1985)—He could do it all. He was a great actor and director with one of the most uniquely dramatic voices, which insured his fame in radio as well. Remember the "War of the Worlds" broadcast that frightened everyone? He won awards for such classics as *Citizen Kane*, which is still studied by film students today. No Hollywood collection is complete without his signature. He died in 1985, but was always a gracious signer, with his signature worth around $75, and signed photographs at $200, although *Citizen Kane* images sell at $300 and up. A couple of documents have surfaced and sold in the $500-600 range, as have a very few letters.
Scarcity Index—★★★

**Mae West** (1893-1980)—Big, bosomy, and brassy, Mae West is a unique screen presence. She wrote and starred in her own stage plays, including one entitled *Sex* that she was arrested for performing. In her first film appearance, her writing ability launched her career when she wrote the line to a hat check girl who, seeing her fur and diamonds, exclaims, "Goodness, those are beautiful," to which West replies, "Goodness had nothing to do with it." Her quotes have made it into dictionaries and quotation books, with her most famous being "Come up and see me sometime." In an era of prudism, she stood out like a madam in the doorway of a bordello beckoning her fans to come have fun with her. She came out of retirement in 1970 to star as a madam in the film *Myra Breckinridge* to rave reviews. West was 77 at the time, and in 1978, at the age of 85, she played opposite Timothy Dalton in *Sextette*. In her retirement years she would sporadically sign fan mail. After her death, her personal belongings were auctioned off, which included approximately 200 personal checks that sell in the $150 range, with her signature worth $100. Signed photographs bring $250 and up, depending on the image.
**Scarcity Index—★★★**

**Robin Williams** (1952-    )—One of the funniest men on the planet is also one of the friendliest with fans, which has kept his authentic signature affordable at $25, with photographs at $60. However, he uses secretaries to sign his mail, so BE CAREFUL. One quick way to distinguish a secretarial signature from Williams' is by checking to see if the signed photograph has an extra line, in addition to the signature written on it, such as "Carpe Diem" or "There's No Face Like Foam." While humorous, and originally conceived by the comedian, these are only written by secretaries. Another popular signed image is as the wisecracking "Genie" in Disney's animated *Aladdin* series of films. Memorable films include *Mrs. Doubtfire*; *Good Morning, Vietnam*; and *Dead Poets Society*.
**Scarcity Index—★**

**Bruce Willis** (1955-    )—One of the most difficult of the modern actors to get to sign, Willis has, on occasion, even taken a photograph from a fan and signed a fake name to it such as "Bill Clinton," before handing it back. His unpleasant signing habits aside, he is a major action star of such hits as the *Die Hard* trilogy of motion pictures, making him collectible to many. What do you do? You pay the price for one of those scarce times he is in the mood to sign (normally at Planet Hollywood openings). His signature sells for $50, with a signed photograph (preferably from *Die Hard*) selling for $150 plus. Documents and letters have yet to surface.
**Scarcity Index—★★★**

**Natalie Wood** (1938-1981)—Beautiful and talented—and married to actor Robert Wagner—Natalie Wood would be a must in any Hollywood collection. Her sudden and sad death in an accidental drowning in 1981 makes her signature scarce and valuable at $100, with signed photographs at $250. Her short career has left us with many memorable roles, however, such as in *West Side Story*, and opposite James Dean in *Rebel Without a Cause*. **Scarcity Index—★★★★**

**Fay Wray** (1907-    )—Although she has starred in many motion pictures, Fay Wray will always be remembered for screaming her way to screen immortality in the giant furry paw of "King Kong" in the 1933 classic. Signed photographs from *King Kong* sell for $60, with her signature at $25. Until the last couple of years, she signed her fan mail quite readily, so is not uncommon. **Scarcity Index—★★**

**Ed Wynn** (1886-1966)—Vaudeville, radio, and TV star, this comic did it all, and had a very unique voice that most fans remember even before his face. He won an Academy Award nomination for a serious role in 1959's *The Diary of Anne Frank*, and is well remembered for his laughing role as a friend of Julie Andrews in the 1964 *Mary Poppins*. (He died two years later in 1966.) His signature is worth $75, with signed photographs selling around $150. A few documents have sold in the same $150 range. **Scarcity Index—★★★**

**Roland Young** (1887-1953)—Young was a great character actor who is best remembered and collected for starring in the hilarious *Topper* films. He died in 1953, and is a fairly uncommon signature, selling in the $40-50 range and $100-150 range on photographs. **Scarcity Index—★★★**

# THE LEGENDARY DIRECTORS

★ ★

**Irwin Allen** (1916-1991)—The famous King of Disasters, director/producer Allen made his first "splash" with the 1961 movie *Voyage to the Bottom of the Sea*, which he later brought to TV as a series. During the same several years that it ran on TV, he produced and directed the hit series "Land of the Giants" and "Lost in Space." He next hit box office bucks with the disaster film *The Poseiden Adventure* in 1972, and was Oscar-nominated for his 1974 disaster flick *The Towering Inferno*. He never answered fan mail, making his signature uncommon at $40, with signed photographs at $75. A document relating to an early film project sold for $200 recently.
**Scarcity Index—★★★★**

**Woody Allen** (1935-    )—A great actor (although limited in range) Woody has proven himself to be a greater director of such classics as *Sleeper* and *Annie Hall*. He is a friendly signer when encountered in NYC (where he lives) and has answered fan mail periodically. His signature sells for $20, with photographs selling for $50.
**Scarcity Index—★**

**Tim Burton** (1958-    )—The unique style of director Tim Burton is easily recognized when viewing his body of work so far. 1988's *BeetleJuice* made a name for him, and landed him the job of creating an updated look for Batman in the film starring Michael Keaton. He did the sequel *Batman Returns*, as well as *Edward Scissorhands* in 1990, followed by the critically-acclaimed *Nightmare Before Christmas* in 1993. He is a gracious signer, although a shy man in person, with the most collectible images being scenes from *Nightmare Before Christmas*, selling at $50, with his signature at $20.
**Scarcity Index—★★**

**Frank Capra** (1897-1991)—Director Capra became so identified with happy endings and sweet, heart-tugging plot lines that his films were dubbed "Capra-Corn" by the critics. Corny or not, they are seen as classics today. He was responsible for such films as *It Happened One Night* (Oscar win), *Mr. Deeds Goes to Town* and *You Can't Take It With You* (Oscar). Ironically, a box office flop when first released, *It's a Wonderful Life* would become a Christmas classic. He was a friendly signer in person, and signed much fan mail in his retirement years, keeping his signature affordable at $35, with signed photographs at $75. Some typed letters have sold in the $100-plus range, depending on content.
Scarcity Index—★★

**Merian C. Cooper** (1893-1973)—Famed producer/director Cooper will always be remembered for his classic 1933 *King Kong*. He went on to head RKO Pictures after David O'Selznik left and, in 1952, he won a Lifetime Achievement Oscar. Not being one of the famous "Faces" like actors/actresses, Cooper was rarely asked to sign autographs. He never signed fan mail after his retirement, making his signature quite scarce. The signature alone can run $200 with letters, photographs, and documents all being even less commonly encountered. A Typed Letter Signed in full by Cooper recently sold for $400.
Scarcity Index—★★★★

**Cecil B. Demille** (1881-1959)—One of the few directors to make the transition from silent films to talkies. In fact, he did 50 silents and 19 talkies. His largely over budgeted Biblical extravaganzas will undoubtably always be remembered. In 1956, his final film *The Ten Commandments*, starring Charlton Heston as "Moses," garnered Oscar nominations as a fitting tribute to both a great film and a great career. Signatures run around $125, with typed letters on his stationery running around $250, as well as a number of business checks that surfaced a few years ago. Signed photographs are a bit scarcer, selling for around $300.
Scarcity Index—★★★

**Walt Disney** (1901-1966)—Many volumes have been published about the King of Cartoons. Walter Elias Disney pioneered film animation. He created the first talking cartoon ("Steamboat Willie") and the first motion picture length cartoon (*Snow White*). He first mixed live actors with cartoons in *Mary Poppins* and *Song of the South* and he built the largest theme parks along the way. He was a friendly signer in person, although he never signed his own fan mail. In person he had a habit of carrying artwork and cards that had already been signed by one of his artists for him. His authentic signature is scarce and sells for over $1000 currently, with signed photographs selling at $3500, and documents selling for even more than photographs. A few business checks have hit the market in the $3000-4000 range. The rarest form of his signature seems to be handwritten letters, as he usually typed all of his correspondence. He was actually more of an inventive genius than an accomplished artist, and hated to be asked by people to dash off a sketch of his most famous creation, "Mickey Mouse." On the rare times that he did a crude drawing and signed it, these pieces have sold for $10,000 and up, depending on their size and detail of the drawing. More often than not, you will encounter a secretary's or artist's signature rather than an authentic Disney. He only signed documents with his full name, and often signed letters simply "Walt," which are worth much less than those signed in full.

**Scarcity Index—★★★★**

**Federico Fellini** (1920-1993)—An Oscar-winning director for foreign films, his style is so famous, that it is taught in film workshops and mimicked today by other aspiring directors. His most famous film (winning him his third Oscar) *Eight and a Half* was, in fact, a film about a director launching his first movie effort. This film is said to have influenced many up and coming directors, such as Woody Allen, who has said so in the press. The year of his death he received a Lifetime Achievement Oscar to add to his earlier wins. Rarely visiting the United States, he is a scarce signature valued at $50 and $100 on photographs. **Scarcity Index**—★★★

**Jim Henson** (1936-1990)—Although not an actor in the strict sense of the word, Henson has certainly started an acting dynasty with his cuddly creations called the "Muppets." He and partner Frank Oz did most of the voices for the characters, and, by 1969, his muppets were regulars on the children's show "Sesame Street." He won several Emmy awards while on "Sesame Street," as he would do later on his own TV series "The Muppet Show" and HBO's "Fraggle Rock." His production team even made the creatures that grace films like *The Flintstones* and *Dark Crystal*. There was even a Saturday morning cartoon show called "The Muppet Babies" and one character, "Kermit the Frog," had a top ten hit song "The Rainbow Connection." Another character, "Miss Piggy," currently stars with supermodels in TV commercials. Shortly after his untimely death from pnemonia in 1990, Henson's heirs sold the Muppet rights to media giant Disney. He often signed fan mail for people, usually in green ink (homage to Kermit?). His signature sells currently for $75, with signed photographs (depicting his characters around him) selling at $250. **Scarcity Index**—★★★

**Alfred Hitchcock** (1899-1980)—Without a doubt, Hitchcock was the Master of Suspense, as his famous body of work shows. Classics like *Psycho, Vertigo,* and *The Birds* will always keep him collectible. He often did small self-caricatures of his famous profile, as shown in the opening sequence of his TV series. These drawings were most often about 3" x 5" in size selling for around $500 today. However, the larger the image, the more costly the sketch. His signature sells for about $250 and signed photographs sell for around $600. Typed letters often surface, signed with his nickname "Hitch," but being an abbreviated form of his name, they are less valuable—unless they have unusually good content.

**Scarcity Index—★★★**

**Elia Kazan** (1909-    )—*On the Waterfront, East of Eden,* and *A Streetcar Named Desire* are just a few reasons why this director will always be collected. He has often signed for fans until the last two years, most probably due to advanced age. His signature is still a great buy at about $20, with signed photographs at $50.

**Scarcity Index—★★**

**Ernst Lubitsch** (1892-1947)—Famous for his romantic operettas starring such actresses as Norma Shearer, Mary Pickford, and others. In 1935, he became head of production for Paramount where he made the Marlene Dietrich classic, *Angel.* In 1939, *Ninotchka,* starring Greta Garbo, would continue to seal his reputation as a great director. *To Be or Not to Be* in 1942 was another career high for Ernst, with his last film (and fifth heart attack) in 1947. A scarce signature running around $100, with signed photographs at about $200.

**Scarcity Index—★★★★**

**George Lucas** (1944-  )—Director Francis Ford Coppola loved what he saw in student film director Lucas, and persuaded Universal to produce the young filmmaker's first effort called *American Graffitti*. It earned the studio lots of money, launched a half dozen young actors to stardom, and gave Lucas two Oscar nods. He went to work in earnest on his next project that, ironically, Universal turned down, but 20th Century Fox wisely picked up. *Star Wars* made Lucas and his newly formed ILM (Industrial Light and Magic) team overnight successes. It had two sequels, and is, due to its recent re-release, one of the highest grossing films of all time, domestically. He is currently working on a three-picture prequel to the trilogy already filmed. As if the *Star Wars* empire was not enough, he went on to create the character "Indiana Jones" that has had a string of hit movies starring Harrison Ford. His ILM team has done special effects work for dozens of other movies as well. He is a kind signer in person, although shy, and employs secretaries to sign his voluminous fan mail. Therefore, his signature is uncommon, selling at $75 on photographs, and $35 as a signature.
Scarcity Index—★★★

**Penny Marshall** (1942-  )—Born in 1942 in the Bronx (as anyone who ever heard her speak may attest to), Marshall already had a famous older brother in director/producer Garry Marshall who gave her her first acting role as Jack Klugman's secretary on his show "The Odd Couple." From that show, she soon starred in another one of big brother's productions as "Laverne" in "Laverne and Shirley" from 1976-1983. After that show, she decided to pursue directing, and with great results. In 1988, she earned wide respect for directing Tom Hanks in the film *Big*, and in 1992, hit a home run with *A League of Their Own*. Her latest directing job was the Whitney Houston movie *The Preacher's Wife*. She is a shy signer, but will sign fan mail (and in person on occasion), making her signature a bit uncommon, selling at $30, with signed photographs (Laverne) selling at $50. A few documents have sold in the $75-100 range.
Scarcity Index—★★★

**Sam Peckinpah** (1925-1984)—Cinema critics either lionized or persecuted Peckinpah for his unique brand of filming. He was famous (or infamous) for a slow-motion sequence he employed during violent scenes. Critics dubbed his style "ballet violence," but it is a trademark that has been widely copied. His breakthrough film was *The Wild Bunch*, where his style is most evident, as it had a feel unlike western films that preceded it. He found a kindred spirit in actor Steve McQueen and directed him in *Junior Bonnor*, which made McQueen a star, and directed him in his classic film *The Getaway*. He rarely signed, and was rarely recognized in person, making his signature quite rare. A signature sells at $75, with signed photographs at $150. A couple of documents have sold in the $150 range as well.
Scarcity Index—★★★★

**Mack Sennett** (1880-1960)—Sennett pioneered and was the "King Director" during the slapstick era of Hollywood—Chaplin, Keystone Kops, Buster Keaton—you name it, he directed them, or gave them their start in film. The list of stars he discovered would be impressive enough after Chaplin, but he also gave starts to Gloria Swanson, Roscoe "Fatty" Arbuckle, Wallace Beery, Carole Lombard, Bing Crosby, and W.C. Fields. In 1937, he won an Honorary Oscar for Lifetime Achievement and retired. He never signed fan mail and rarely signed in person. Usually only a rare signed letter or document surfaces, and these sell for $1000 and up.
Scarcity Index—★★★★★

**Steven Spielberg** (1947-  )—Director extraordinaire, Spielberg has directed 6 of the top 10 grossing films of all time. A master storyteller, he brought us *ET*, *Jaws*, *Close Encounters of the Third Kind*, *Gremlins*, *Jurassic Park*, and *Schindler's List*, to name but a few. He co-directed, with pal George Lucas, on the string of *Indiana Jones* films. There is no end in sight for this supremely talented man. He is a MUST in a Hollywood collection, and although he does not sign his mail (he sends a pre-printed oblong card showing himself with *ET*), he does sign in person when asked, with his autograph selling at $50, and signed photographs at $100. A couple of documents have sold in the $200 range.
Scarcity Index—★★★

# COLLECTIBLE MOVIE CASTS

## "He Swings Through the Trees:"
## The Legacy of Tarzan

Over 85 years ago, author Edgar Rice Burroughs published his first "Tarzan" story in a magazine called *The All-Story*. Nearly everyone the world over recognizes the name "Tarzan" today, and Burroughs went on to spawn an empire of books, movies, merchandise, clubs, TV shows, and acting careers.

"Tarzan" incidentally means "White Skin" in ape language, but today it means adventure—swinging through the trees—a superhero whose skills were more believable instead of super-heroes that based their skills on gadgets and super-weapons. Tarzan used brute strength, character, and courage to overcome evil forces.

Although Burroughs died in 1950, he had already written 67 novels; twenty-six were about Tarzan. His creation was already appearing in newspapers in comic strip form, as well as his own series of comic books. Tarzan was on TV and radio at the same time and Tarzan was sponsoring every piece of conceivable merchandise he could get his rugged face on, from loaves of bread to children's notebooks.

Burroughs lived in isolation on his own 540-acre ranch in the San Fernando Valley, but as a city began to flourish around his home, the locals named it Tarzana in honor of their founder.

Over 45 motion pictures have been made with Tarzan as the lead, starring some 18 actors. The first picture in 1918 was a silent film starring an ex-police officer named Elmo Lincoln. Actors Gene Pollar and Dempsey Tabler played him after Lincoln, but the first truly athletic Tarzan would hit the screen with the fourth actor to play him, Jim Pierce.

Pierce played Tarzan only once in *Tarzan and the Golden Lion*, but he found a greater role in Tarzan lore when he married Burroughs' daughter, Joan. Joan and Jack would go on to play Tarzan and Jane on radio for 15 years.

Late in 1928, Frank Merrill, a gymnast, played Tarzan (twice), but in 1932, the most famous Tarzan of all took over the jungle, Johnny Weissmuller. Actress Maureen O'Sullivan played Jane opposite Weissmuller, and his first film was one of the top ten grossing films of the year.

MGM stayed to the formula of a jungle savant, whereas Burroughs had written that Tarzan eventually learns several languages and even lives in a mansion, not the trees. So, ironically, being a commercial success was not enough for Burroughs, who decided to film his own version, which he felt more closely resembled his written creation. He cast Herman Brix, an Olympic medalist, to play the lead in it. Brix, who later changed his stage name to Bruce Bennett, played a more dignified Tarzan, and is collected by autograph fans to this day for his portayal. Brix, redubbed Bennett, left the jungle after these two films and went on to a long career as a character actor opposite many great actors and actresses, including Joan Crawford and Humphrey Bogart.

Brix would not be the last Olympic medalist to play the jungle lord. Buster Craabe would swing from the trees after winning Gold medals in swimming. Later, Glen Morris, who won a Gold in the decathalon, would play Tarzan as well.

Most Tarzan autograph collectors want to collect every actor who has ever donned the loincloth.

Elmo Lincoln was first and is the rarest autograph, selling for several hundred dollars for a signature. Pierce's signature is valued today at $100, and Weissmuller's sells at $150. Gene Pollar and Dempsey Tabler, mentioned earlier, sell for around $150 each and are scarce. Frank Merrill played Tarzan next, and is worth about $150 as a signature.

Next to Weissmuller, Buster Craabe is probably the most collected Tarzan. His signature sells at $60, with signed photographs as Tarzan selling at $150. Craabe played "Buck Rogers" in early movies, too, and is highly collected as that image, as well.

Herman Brix (aka Bruce Bennett) still signs at occasional Tarzan conventions, and sells at $40 on photographs, and $15 for a signature alone. He often signs both his real and stage name on photographs.

Glenn Morris, mentioned earlier, sells for $100 as a signature. He died in 1972, but had signed very little prior to his death.

Lex Barker played Tarzan in the late 1940s and early 1950s,

and, like Morris, died in 1972. His signature sells at $50.

Gordon Scott played Tarzan next, and is considered by collectors to be one of the top three actors to play him. Fortunately, Scott still does trade shows and signs fan mail. He has been signing much material for over a decade now, keeping his signature at $15, and signed photographs as Tarzan at $50.

Denny Miller, a former basketball star, swung on the vine after Scott. Miller played him only once in a 1959 movie, but does have the distinction of being the only blonde to play Tarzan. He signs fan mail and at shows today, which has, for years, kept his signature affordable at $15, and signed Tarzan images at $35.

Jock Mahoney played Tarzan first in the 1960s in two movies. Mahoney had been a stunt double for such western stars as Gene Autry and Charles Starrett, and was actress Sally Field's stepfather. Although he died in a 1989 car accident, he had been a friendly signer for years, and his signatures now sell for $30, with signed photographs at $75.

Mike Henry played Tarzan several times in the late 1960s and still acts in small TV and movie roles today. He is, though, a tougher signature to acquire, running around $35.

Ron Ely is well-remembered for playing Tarzan on TV for two years, and in movies, but does not recall those days fondly, and hates signing Tarzan images, making a photograph sell at $75, with signatures alone at $35.

In 1981, they re-made the first Tarzan movie with Bo Derek as Jane and football player Miles O'Keefe as Tarzan. He does not answer fan mail, but has signed in person for fans. Uncommon, his signatures sell at $35, with signed photographs at $65.

Christopher Lambert is best remembered today for the series of *Highlander* films he starred in opposite Sean Connery. But he played Tarzan in the 1985 movie titled *Greystoke: The Legend of Tarzan*. Because he lives in Europe and does not answer fan mail, he is tough to get, selling at $30 as a signature, and $65 on a Tarzan photograph.

Joe Lara played Tarzan in the 1989 movie *Tarzan in Manhattan*, but the movie did poorly, and his signature is less in demand, selling at $15, with photographs at $30.

To build a complete collection of Tarzans would require time and patience, but can still be accomplished without selling the family home. It is a rich and rewarding cinema collecting goal. Would a completist want Carol Burnett's signature because of her Tarzan parody sketch and her trademark Tarzan yell?

# Dead and Loving It—
# The History of Dracula in the Cinema

One of the most collected areas today for entertainment autograph enthusiasts is the genre of horror stars. An entire book could be written on just this subject, so, in the interest of introducing you to the collecting possibilities of this genre, I will go over a listing of all of the stars who have ever played "Count Dracula" in the cinema, which is a very collectible category.

Most people with a little bit of knowledge in the horror field believe that one man typified Dracula above all others— Bela Lugosi. You must be careful that you do not buy a Mrs. Lugosi, as his wife signed nearly all of his fan mail during his career. He, unfortunately, got hooked on morphine and other painkillers, which eventually killed him while filming a B movie for young director Edward Wood—a movie that has a cult-like status today—called *Planet Nine From Outerspace*.

But, let's start at the beginning, Lugosi was typecast to play heavies and vampires from the start of his career. Hungarian born and raised (the accent was real), he came to America with high hopes of being a dashing leading man—not unrealistic hopes, as he had already become Hungary's number one silent film star—and had worked on stage there since he was a teen after extensive studies at the Budapest Academy of Theatrical Arts. In America, he was cast almost immediately in the Broadway version of *Dracula* in 1927, which he played for more than two years, including a national tour. Lugosi got rave reviews.

Hollywood had tried a vampire flick already, but was, at the time, unwilling to pay the author of *Dracula*, Bram Stoker, a licensing fee. So, they did a knockoff silent film called *Nosferatu* with a rat-like-looking makeup job on the actor—not the dramatic caped Count that Stoker wrote about.

In 1929, when Universal Studios was ready to pay royalties for Stoker's creation (which, by the way, was based loosely on a real Count named "Vlad the Impaler," whose castle in Hungary still stands), they chose Lon Chaney, Sr., instead of Lugosi. (Lugosi, at the time, wasn't as well-known as Chaney.) Chaney was Universal's biggest star at the time, and was billed as the "Man of a 1,000 Faces" for both his makeup and acting expertise. He appeared in films such as *Phantom of the Opera*, *The Hunchback of Notre Dame*, and *London After Dark*, which was actually a story about a deranged killer who only acts like a vampire to fool police, but is not one. The movie was more a psychological thriller than horror movie, but it proved to Universal that they were on to a good thing. They announced aquiring the rights to the novel *Dracula* and cast Chaney to play it. Filming was to begin in 1930, when tragedy struck, and Chaney died of cancer.

The studios were stuck and filming was about to begin. They decided to go with the unknown actor that had been playing the Count to packed houses on stage, Bela Lugosi. It is hard to imagine anyone else in the role today.

Lugosi's thick accent hurt him time after time when auditioning for those leading men roles he so wanted to sink his teeth into. But, the same accent helped him play the Transylvanian Count.

The movie was a hit, so Universal offered him the lead in the next horror novel they optioned, *Frankenstein*. But Lugosi felt he had to do something to stop further typecasting, so he turned the role down. It went to another newcomer who Lugosi would have a lifelong feud with, Boris Karloff.

After two years of only getting supporting roles, Lugosi reluctantly returned to Universal in a film (1934's *The Black Cat*) that paired him with Karloff.

In 1943, after years of watching his career slide downhill, he actually played the part he'd once turned down—"Frankenstein," in the movie *Frankenstein Meets the Wolfman*. The same year he played a vampire again in *Return of the Vampire*, and his career continued to spiral. He did a comic turn as Dracula in 1948's *Abbott and Costello Meet Frankenstein*, but his career was nearly over—and in the process, he'd become addicted to morphine. He did check into a rehabilitation clinic in 1955 to kick his addiction, but it had already taken a toll on his physical health. Per his personal instructions, Lugosi was buried in the cape he wore so often as Dracula.

A signature of Lugosi is worth $450 currently, with a signed photograph in a non-Dracula role worth $1500. A signed "Dracula" photograph is worth $3500. A document sold recently for $2000. Letters are scarce, and pricey as well.

Boris Karloff, while a MUST for horror collectors, never played the famous Count. His signature is valued at $350 today, with signed portraits selling at $600—although a "Frankenstein" image would hit $1000 plus. Quite a few acting documents relating to voice work on radio and small plays have hit the market, selling at around $600 each.

Karloff died in 1969, the year he narrated the now annual classic cartoon "How the Grinch Stole Christmas."

When Lon Chaney, Sr., died, his acting son, Creighton Chaney, changed his name legally to Lon Chaney, Jr., in tribute to his father. He had tried being a distinguished actor like dear old dad, but along with the name change, he was irresistable to Universal Studios, who were in search of a new horror star. He played Dracula once in the 1943 *Son of Dracula*, but gave more convincing performances in a series of *Wolfman* films.

He died in 1973 with his signature valued at $300 plus currently, and signed photographs in non-horror roles at $550. As "Wolfman," a signed photograph would bring $750 plus. A couple of documents have sold in the same $700-plus range.

Actor John Carradine would play the Count next in the Universal film *House of Frankenstein* and *House of Dracula* in 1944 and 1945. He played other sinister roles in other horror movies, but for our collecting purposes, these two films added him to the list of those that donned the cape. He died in 1988, and had signed some fan mail before his death, but is still an uncommon signature valued at $75, with signed photographs at $200—and as Dracula, which are rare at $500 when one last sold.

The 1950s and 1960s horror films took on a different feel. Instead of relying on true Hitchcockian-style suspense and horror, they became more graphic in their urge to get a scream from the audience. In large part, one B movie director—Hammer—would dominate the field for 15 years with a handful of stars producing the gorier and bloodier forerunners to our modern day blood epics like *Halloween*, *Jason*, and *Friday the 13th* movies.

Most all of Hammers' *Dracula* films starred one Brit by the name of Christopher Lee. Lee once said of he and frequent co-star Peter Cushing that "He and I have made so many horror films together that people think we live in a cave together." Cushing, played the sophisticated "Dr. Helsing" in most of the Hammer classics, forever trying to drive that stake through Lee's vampire heart.

In 1958, Lee played the Count in *Horror of Dracula*, and the "Mummy" in Hammer's next film. He even played the assassin "Scaramunga" in the James Bond film *The Man with the Golden Gun*. He played "Dracula," however, in more movies than any other actor, and has been a gracious signer ever since he retired in the late 1970s. He has not signed fan mail for some time now—and now lives in England, which makes it tougher to reach him. A signature sells at $35, with signed "Dracula," "Mummy," "Frankenstein," or "Scaramunga" photographs (the only real collectible images) selling at $100.

Peter Cushing did play Dracula once, instead of the pursuer Dr. Helsing he played so often, which makes him a must in this collection—but he is a must in any horror collection, at any rate. He was a friendly signer who even signed fan mail within weeks of his death in 1995. He lived in England and his last film role was in the classic film *Star Wars* as the "Admiral of the Death Star Station." Signed photographs in horror roles or the *Star Wars* role sell for $100, with signatures alone at $45.

No horror collection is complete without a Vincent Price signature, but he never played the Count on screen. He signed for any fan who asked, and answered fan mail the last years of his life, even signing self-caricatures for fans that are very collectible today.

The only other actor, besides Lugosi, to play Dracula on Broadway and the movies was actor Frank Langella. Langella has, on occasion, signed fan mail, and will usually sign when approached in person, with his signature selling for $30, and signed photographs as "Dracula" selling at $60. A couple of early documents from Langella's career have sold at $150.

The horror genre as a whole can provide an entire lifetime of collecting pleasures. We hope with this synopsis of just one element of it—*Dracula*—we have whet your appetite for more.

# Follow the Yellow Brick Road— Collecting the Cast of *The Wizard of Oz*

One of the most popular of all the movie casts being collected today is that of the wonderful *The Wizard of Oz*, which debuted to lackluster ticket sales in 1939. Even performing badly at the box office, the film still made a hit song out of "Over the Rainbow," and a star out of Judy Garland.

The cast is a tricky one to collect, but it can be done. The cast of 200 performers who portrayed the "Munchkins" in the film may be an unrealistic goal, but you can secure quite a few, including the more prominent ones in the film.

Judy Garland is naturally the cornerstone of an *Oz* collection, and there is a wealth of great material out there to buy on her. A signature will cost around $400, with signed photographs selling at around $900. One of her ex-husbands, Sid Luft, with whom she had a daughter (Lorna), sold some of Judy's personal checks some time back at $800 each, and several documents have traded hands in the past couple of years at $1000 and up, depending on content.

To date, none of the major star's contracts have surfaced from this particular film. Props and costumes from the classic film also bring top prices, with a pair of her ruby slippers being the Holy Grail to most collectors. Only seven pairs ever existed and the last pair sold at auction many years ago for over $250,000. In a famous auction back in 1970 on the lot of MGM, they sold a lion suit worn by the "Cowardly Lion" for $3300; it sold for over $100,000 in 1996 privately. Michael Jackson, the singer, ponied up over $60,000 for the hourglass used by the "Wicked Witch" in the film, and her hat and broom have sold in years past, as have ten of the gingham dresses worn in the film by Judy, the last recorded sale of one being $40,000.

*The Wizard of Oz*—based on a book originally written by author Frank Baum—is loved the world over and anything associated with it is collectible.

But the film did not get released to TV until 1956, and it would be a time before it became the classic it is today. Sadly, quite a few cast members were already dead, making it impossible to get a signed photograph of them in character.

Judy Garland's signed photographs as "Dorothy" are very rare, as Judy died of a drug overdose in 1969. The last recorded sale of such a photograph brought $4000.

Then there is the irrepressible main cast she encounters along the yellow brick road to the Emerald City. First is the "Scarecrow of Oz" played by brilliant dancer Ray Bolger. Bolger, a very friendly signer who attended *Oz* conventions, signed posters, and photographs for autograph dealers, and signed fan mail up until his death in 1987. (He was, in fact, the last major cast member to die.)

Because his signature is not uncommon, you can still buy one for around $60, with signed photographs as the Scarecrow (he often wrote "Scarecrow of Oz" on them along with his name) selling at $200. These continue to rise in value and are probably a good investment.

Next, Dorothy encounters the "Tin Man of Oz" who was originally cast by actor Buddy Ebsen of "Beverly Hillbillies" fame, but after filming began, he had a terrible allergic reaction to the aluminum dust used in the makeup, and was replaced by actor Jack Haley. Haley died in 1979, and had done an appearance or two just before his death. He was a friendly signer, too, and signed "Tin Man" photographs exist, selling at $350 on average today, with his signature at $125. Several signed business checks have surfaced that have been selling at $150 each.

Dorothy met the loveable "Cowardly Lion" last of all, played brilliantly by vaudevillian Bert Lahr. Lahr died in 1967; therefore, it would be rare if any photographs of him as the lion exist. None have traded hands in years if so. A regular signed portrait of Lahr sells at $600, with a signature selling at $300. A couple of documents have sold in the $500 range.

The foursome get roughed up a bit by the villain in the story played magnificently by Margaret Hamilton as the "Wicked Witch of the West."

Margaret played "Cora," the Maxwell House coffee spokesperson in commercials up until her death in 1985. She answered fan mail, and signed for fans until the end. Her signature sells at $100, with signed photographs as the "Wicked Witch" selling in the $350-400 range. She often signed "Maggie" or with only her initials or "WWW," meaning "Wicked Witch of the West," and, while authentic, these are worth quite a bit less. A few documents and letters have sold in the $500 range in the past two years.

Hamilton's wicked sister was killed by the falling house early on, and we are only aquainted with one other witch—Glinda, the "Good Witch of the South," played by retired actress and Ziegfield showgirl, Billie Burke.

Burke signed a lot for fans in earlier years, so her signature is available for around $200 with signed photographs selling around $300. She died in 1970, which makes finding a Glinda-signed photograph rare as hens' teeth. One did sell several years ago for $1500.

The great and magical "Wizard of Oz" himself was played by veteran stage actor Frank Morgan. Morgan died in 1949, before any other cast members, making him one of the scarcest three signatures to find. You will NOT find a signed photograph in character, nor does one probably exist. A regular portrait-signed photograph sells at $700, with his signature at $400 plus. A document sold last year for $600.

Dorothy's Aunt and Uncle are the rarest two signatures to obtain because they were character actors hardly recognized on the street by collectors, and they both passed away years ago without answering fan mail.

The Uncle was played by Charley Grapewin, who died in 1956, and when encountered, his signature sells for $350 plus. No documents or signed photographs are even known of at this time. Dorothy's Auntie Em was played by character actress Clara Blandick who died in 1962 (She committed suicide.) Again, no  photographs have surfaced of Blandick, but signatures in autograph albums have surfaced selling for $350 plus, like Grapewin. Last year, an autograph firm uncovered and sold at auction the only document to surface at $1200.

There were nearly 215 midgets who played various townspeople and other Munchkin roles. Meinhart Raabe is still alive and a popular signer on the *Oz* show circuit—he played the "Munchkin Coroner" who gives the Death Deed to Dorothy for the witch who was killed when her house fell in Oz. A signed photograph as Coroner sells at around $40. Jerry Maren offered Dorothy a lollipop and sang that famous song. He also does conventions today, and his signed photographs are around $30.

Only a handful (less than twenty) of the "Munchkin" actors are alive today, but most do conventions and sign for fans. At one show years ago, 26 munchkins, the most ever assembled, signed photographs that sell for around $600 (signed by all 26) today. Many other photographs, signed by combinations of them, have sold over the years.

The director of the film was the incomparable Victor Fleming, who also did the final credited direction on the classic *Gone with the Wind* that same year. He died in 1949, and is a rare signature today, selling for $1000 on a photograph, and $400 as a signature alone.

Join the thousands of other autograph collectors that are following the Yellow Brick Road!

# These Autographs are . . .
## *Gone with the Wind*

*The Wizard of Oz* and *Gone with the Wind* are easily the most collected movie casts with autograph collectors. Unlike *Oz*, however, many of the original motion picture contracts signed by stars of *GWTW* recently surfaced at auction.

Clark Gable never won an Academy Award for the film. In fact, his only Academy Award win was for the 1934 classic *It Happened One Night*, which sold at auction for over $600,000 in 1997. (Steven Spielberg bought it.) Two years ago, over $550,000 was paid at auction for Vivien Leigh's Oscar as "Scarlett O'Hara" in *GWTW*.

Author Margaret Mitchell only wrote one novel her entire life, *Gone with the Wind*. Literally thousands of toys, perfume, puzzles, clothing, and other licensed items have sold in the last 50 plus years since the film's release.

It is difficult but fun to collect all of the stars from this classic film—difficult because so many people appeared in the film and most are deceased.

The two principle stars, Clark Gable and Vivien Leigh, ("Scarlett" and "Rhett") are the most collectible. Gable died in 1961 just weeks after finishing the film the Misfits with actress Marilyn Monroe. A few years ago, about 400 of Gable's personal checks were found in an old home. Those checks sell at around $400 each currently. His signature sells at $275, with signed photographs selling at $700.

Vivien Leigh passed away in 1967 and was a friendly signer until her death. Vivien's signature sells at $350 currently, with signed photographs at $650, unless the photograph is as "Scarlett," which sells easily at $1500.

Vivien's sisters in the film were played by Evelyn Keyes and Ann Rutherford. Both are alive, and still sign for fans today. Photographs in character sell at $40, and signatures at $20.

Like any Southern plantation in the Civil War era, Scarlett had a maid and a "Mammy," played by black character actresses Butterfly McQueen ("Prissy") and Hattie McDaniel ("Mammy").

Hattie McDaniel died in 1952, when America sadly was still a very segregated place, making her signature quite rare, selling at $550, and $1200 on a photograph. In 1940, she was the first black to win an Academy Award.

Butterfly McQueen died tragically in a house fire in 1996. Prior to her death, McQueen charged for her signature, but signed quite a bit over the years, with her signature selling now at $60, and signed photographs as "Prissy" selling at $125. Hundreds of her personal checks were sold to collectors (many by her) which currently sell for $100 each.

Another very rare signature is George Reeves (TV's "Superman"), who played twins in the film. He was always a tough signer, and committed suicide in 1959, making him even rarer. A signature sells for $700 easily, with signed photographs selling at $1500.

Actor Fred Crane played "Brent Tarleton" in the film, and is still alive and making appearances, with a signature selling at $25, and photographs at $50.

"Gerald O'Hara," played by actor Thomas Mitchell, was a friendly signer, but having died in 1962, his signature is very scarce today, selling at $250, and $500 on photographs.

Character actor Victor Jory played "Jonas Wilkerson" in the film and is a more common signature, having died in 1982. He signed frequently for fans, including through fan mail. A Jory signature sells at $75, with signed photographs at $150.

"Ashley Wilkes," who tried for Scarlett's hand in the film, was played by actor Leslie Howard, who sells at $350 as a signature, and $550 as a signed photograph. He died in 1940, shortly after the film's release, in a plane crash.

"Melanie Hamilton" was played by actress Olivia DeHavilland who is still alive and living in Paris. She signed most of her fan mail for years, as well as signing large quantities of photographs for an autograph firm. Her photographs in character sell at $50, with her signature alone selling at $25.

"Charles Hamilton" was played by actor Rand Brooks, who still signs fan mail today, with in-character photographs selling at $40, and signatures at $20.

Child star Cammie King played "Bonnie Butler" in the film, and still signs photographs today selling at $40, with signatures at $20.

"Ukelele Ike," who was also the voice of "Jiminy Cricket" in *Pinnochio*, played a "Reminiscent Soldier" in *GWTW*. Edward's signature sells at $100, with signed photographs at $200. He died in 1971.

Roscoe Ates played a "Convalescent Soldier" in the film. He died in 1962, and is a fairly scarce signature at $100.

Character actor Louis Jean Heydt played a "Hungry Soldier" in the film. Heydt is a fairly scarce signature, like most character actors, and he died in 1960, keeping his price at $125 plus.

Isabell Jewell, who died in 1972, played "Emmy Slattery," and is a rare signature, selling at $250 plus.

"Tom, A Yankee Captain" was played by famed western actor Ward Bond, who was always a friendly signer for fans, but having died in 1960, is getting scarcer year by year. A Bond signature sells at $100, with signed photographs at $200.

Character actor Eddie "Rochester" Anderson, who played Jack Benny's sidekick for years, also appeared in *GWTW*, playing "Uncle Peter." Anderson sells at around $75 for a signature.

Actress Jane Darwell, who died in 1960 after appearing as the "Bird Lady" in *Mary Poppins*, played "Ms. Merriweather" in the film, and sells at $125 for a signature, and $250 for signed photographs.

Laura Hope Crews played "Aunt Pittypat" in the film. She died in 1942, and is one of the rarer signatures, bringing $300.

Harry Davenport is another rare autograph from the film. He played "Dr. Meade" and died in 1949.

To round out the cast are even rarer character actor/actresses that sell depending on the market at the time. Prices can't be estimated since they so rarely turn up, but most would sell in the $100-300 range.

"Big Sam"—Everett Brown
"Elijah"—Zack Williams
"Pork"—Oscar Polk
"Ellen O'Hara"—Barbara O'Neill
"John Wilkes"—Howard Hickman
"India Wilkes"—Alicia Rhett
"Frank Kennedy"—Carol Nye
"Cathleen Calvert"—Marcella Martin
"Phil Meade"—Jackie Moran
"Old Levi"—William McClaine
"Fanny Elsing"—Terry Shero
"Maybelle Merriweather"—Mary Anderson
"Rene Picard"—Albert Morin
"Mrs. Meade"—Leona Roberts
"Yankee Mayor"—Robert Elliott
"Poker Playing Capt."—George Meeker
"Corporal"—Irving Bacon
"Poker Playing Capt."—Wallis Clark

"Johnny Gallager"—JM Kerrigan
"Yankee Businessman"—Olin Howland
"Renegade"—Yakima Canutt
"Renegade's Companion"—Blue Washington
"Beau Wilkes"—Micky Kuhn
"Carpetbagger Orator"—Adrian Morris
"Bartender"—Lee Phelps
"Bonnie's Nurse"—Lillian Kemble Cooper
"Mounted Officer"—William Bakewell
"Commanding Officer"—Tom Tyler
"Dying Soldier"—John Arledge
"Returning Veteran"—William Stelling
"Seargent"—Ed Chandler
"Wounded Soldier"—George Hackathorne
"Belle Watling"—Ona Munson
"Amputation Case"—Eric Linden
"Yankee Deserter"—Paul Hurst
"Carpetbagger's Friend"—Ernest Whitman

The famous producer of the film is needed for any complete collection. David O'Selznik's signature sells at around $200, with scarcer signed photographs at $350. The director, Victor Fleming (many contributed, but he got screen credit), is rare, and sells for $400, with signed photographs at $1000. Author Margaret Mitchell's is a blue chip autograph selling at $750, with signed photographs at $1500. First editions of the book sell for $4000 in perfect condition, with original dust jacket.

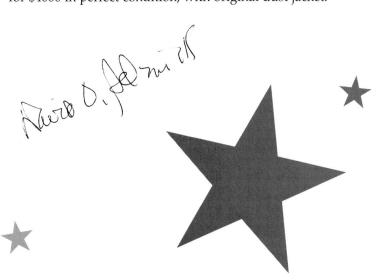

# CASABLANCA

The third most collected movie casts after *The Wizard of Oz* and *Gone with the Wind* is *Casablanca*.

The most expensive element to collect is star Humphrey Bogart that sells for as much as $900 for a single signature.

Paul Henreid, who died only two years ago, sells for around $50 for a signature, and $100 for a signed photograph in character from the film.

Ingrid Bergman, who died many years ago, is $400 on a *Casablanca* photograph, and around $150 for a single signature.

Peter Lorre is rare on *Casablanca* photographs, and a signature runs around $125.

The rarest, and second in value, is that of Dooley Wilson who played "Casablanca Sam," the black pianist to whom Bogart remarked, "Play It Again, Sam." He died many years ago, and his signature is rare (★★★★★) selling for as much as $1500 on a photograph from the film, and $400 for a simple signature.

Claude Rains, who became more famous for playing the "Invisible Man," sells for around the $125-150 range for a signature, with a signed portrait selling for twice that amount. But, as with the others, a signed photograph in character from this film is rare, if it exists at all.

# TV CAST-A-WAYS—
## Collecting Your Favorite TV Casts

Many autograph collectors build collections of their favorite TV cast. There are literally hundreds of shows that have been on TV since its inception that are collected, but for the sake of our space in this first volume, we will discuss the pitfalls of collecting the currently most collected TV casts. We have arrived at our list by asking dozens of dealers in Entertainment autographs, as well as researching magazine articles that profile different TV shows. Of the vintage shows, "Dragnet," "Adam 12," "Sanford and Son," "Maude," "Leave it to Beaver," "The Big Valley," and many more are collected, as well as modern show casts such as "Seinfeld," "Murphy Brown," "E.R.," "Baywatch," and "Friends."

"I Love Lucy" (From 1951-1957)—This is considered by many to be the most watched TV show worldwide. The cast of four should be simple enough to collect, but things are not always what they should be. Lucille Ball's signature is actually the easiest of the four (and last cast member to die) selling at $75, with signed photographs at $250. Husband Desi Arnaz, who died a few years earlier than Lucy, was a friendly signer in retirement, signing much of his fan mail, and selling at just below Lucy's prices. The rub in collecting the cast is the "Mertz's," who lived next door. Vivian Vance, who died in 1979, was a tough signer in person, and rarely signed any fan mail, making her signature scarce. A signature sells for $200, with signed photographs from the TV series much prized at $500 plus. A couple of Vance documents have sold for $300 plus. The toughest signature is that of "Fred Mertz," played by character actor William Frawley. He died shortly after the series ended and was a notoriously tough signer. He hated to sign in person for fans and never signed fan mail. His signature sells for $300 easily, with no signed photographs in character to even document sales on.

**"The Honeymooners"** (From 1955-1956)—Next on the list is "The Honeymooners." Jackie Gleason, Audrey Meadows, Art Carney, and Joyce Randolph played the two couples in what many critics think is the smartest comedy writing on TV still! In fact, years after Gleason's death, and over 25 years after the show was last on TV, a number of "lost episodes" were unearthed and aired on hip cable station MTV, where a new younger audience howled in approval. Gleason used secretaries to sign a lot of his mail, so once again BE CAREFUL on his signature. The other three signed fan mail and at shows until this past year, when we lost actress Audrey Meadows. A signed photograph of the three without Gleason sells at $175, with all four on a photograph at an easy $400 today. Individual signatures are $75 plus for Gleason, and $30 for Meadows, with signatures of the always gracious Art Carney and Joyce Randolph selling at $15 a piece.

**"Gunsmoke"** (From 1955-1975)—"Gunsmoke" was the number one rated western on TV for years. James Arness as "Matt Dillon" spent years signing for fans, although due to age, he has not signed lately. A signed photograph as the "Sheriff" fetches $75, with a signed card at $25. "Miss Kitty" played by deceased actress Amanda Blake sells for around the same amount. A number of her personal checks hit the market, selling quite reasonably, as well. Dennis Weaver and Burt Reynolds still sign much material to this day, and are easy additions to your collection. The tough signatures are actor Ken Curtis as "Festus," who signed much material for fans, but has been dead for some time now, making his signature a bit uncommon. He sells at $40, with signed photographs as "Festus" selling at $100. The rare cast member, and the first to pass away, is "Doc" played by actor Milburn Stone, whose scarce signature sells for $100 currently, with signed photographs being quite rare.

**"Bonanza"** (From 1959-1973)—"Bonanza" is another of the most collectible western TV shows. The cast members are all deceased today. Dan Blocker, who played "Hoss," is the scarcest of this collectible cast's signatures, as he died while filming the show in 1961. A signature sells at $200, with signed images as "Hoss" selling for $500. A portrait would sell for less. Documents and letters are rarer. Actor Lorne Greene and actor Pernell Roberts worked for many years on various other TV shows and movies before each passed away. A "Lorne Greene" signed photograph sells at $100 in character. Actor Michael Landon, who would go on to star in several other series like "Highway to Heaven" and "Little House on the Prairie," died of cancer before signing much fan mail. A signed photograph in character sells for $200, with signatures at $80. Pernell Roberts was a notorious non-signer, with his scarce signature selling for $100. A signed photograph by all four sold for $1200 at auction recently.

**"The Addam's Family"** (From 1964-1966)—Like many cast-signed photographs, you must watch for forgeries on this one! John Astin as "Gomez," Addams has always signed for fans, and is inexpensive at $15 for a signature, and $40 on photographs as "Gomez," which he often adds after his name. Carolyn Jones, who played his wife "Morticia," is quite another matter. She died over ten years ago and was reclusive for years prior to her death. She did, however, sign some fan mail, but so did secretaries. Her own signature, as illustrated here, is very distinctive, fortunately, and not at all like the neat cursive signatures of her secretaries. An authentic "Carolyn Jones" signature sells at $75, with signed photographs as Morticia selling at $250. Lisa Loring played "Wednesday" on the series, and upon growing up, she played in many soap operas. She has been a willing signer, even signing large amounts for autograph dealers. A signed photograph in character sells for $30, with signatures at $15. Kenneth Weatherwax played "Pugsley" on the series, and later, went behind the scenes in Hollywood as a technician. When located job to job, he has on occasion signed for fans, with his signature selling at $40, and signed photographs at $80. Ted Cassidy is one of the two rarest signatures to obtain. He played "Lurch," as well as supplying the hand known as "Thing" on the series. Tragically, Cassidy died in an apartment fire twenty years ago, making his signature quite rare, selling at $150, with signed photographs as "Lurch" (quite rare) selling at $400 plus. Actress Blossom Rock played "Grandmama" and sells as much as Cassidy, due to rarity. Jackie Coogan, who played "The Kid" opposite Charlie Chaplin and in countless shows over the years, played the bald headed "Uncle Fester." He signed fan mail in his retirement years, and sells currently at $40 for signatures, and $125 on a photo. The hairy "Cousin It" was played by tiny actor Felix Silla, who has signed at a few conventions, with those photographs selling at $40. Be wary of an entire cast signed photograph—most dealers think they don't exist. The combination you can hope for is one signed by Astin, Jones, Coogan, and Loring (maybe Weatherwax), and these even sell for $250 plus.

**"The Munsters"** (From 1964-1966)—"The Munsters" is another popularly collected cast. The quirky family who thought everyone else was stranger looking than they were kept a stranglehold on the ratings for years. Fred Gwynne played "Herman Munster" and died three years ago, after playing the judge opposite Joe Pesci in the hit film *My Cousin Vinny*.

Gwynne used secretaries to sign mail often, so BE CAREFUL! His signature sells at $50 today, with signed photographs as Herman Munster, which he was not too fond of signing, selling at $200 plus. Actress Yvonne DeCarlo still signs as "Lilly Munster," and has even signed large quantities for autograph firms, as have every other cast member—Al Lewis as "Grandpa Munster," Butch Patrick as "Eddie," and Pat Priest as "Marilyn." Most signed cast photographs do not have Gwynne on them, and sell at around $150. With an authentic "Gwynne" they would sell for $350 plus.

**"Gilligans Island"** (From 1964-1967)—Like most shows, "Gilligan's Island" does extremely well in syndication, constantly expanding its fan base by adding new and younger viewers. The stars that were stranded after a "three hour tour" were: Jim Backus, Bob Denver, Natalie Schafer, Russell Johnson, Tina Louise, Alan Hale Jr., and Dawn Wells. Jim Backus was an established movie star nearing retirement when he signed on to play "Thurston Howell III." He was also known to millions as the voice behind the cartoon character "Mr. Magoo." Backus was always a friendly signer, even signing fan mail in later years. But he has been dead for a few years now, and his signature is getting more uncommon, selling at $35 with a signed photograph selling at $75. "Thurston's" wife "Lovey" was played by actress Natalie Schaefer, who is also deceased and selling in the same range as Backus. Bob Denver has had two hit TV shows starring first in the "Many Adventures of Dobie Gillis" before becoming first mate on the fated SS Minnow and going down in history as "Gilligan." He still signs some fan mail and appears at the occasional convention. He often signs "Gilligan" under his real name. A signature sells at $20, with signed photographs at $40. Dawn Wells, who played "Mary Ann" on the show, is a frequent guest at nostalgia shows, as is actor Russell Johnson, who played the "Professor." Due to constant signing, both signatures can be had for $15, with signed photographs in character selling at $30. Tina Louise is a friendly signer, but will not sign images as "Ginger" from the show. She feels the series typecast her and hurt her career. You usually must be content buying a signature card for around $20 to matt with a cast photograph. Ten years ago she would sign cast photographs, rather than be the only holdout if all the other characters had signed. Last year, she did a private signing of an artist print that was signed by the living cast members. The hardest signature to find by far is the first member of the cast to die, Alan Hale, Jr. Hale would sign in person for fans at a seafood resturant he owned in retirement, but rarely signed any fan mail. His signature is uncommon, selling at $100 currently. A signed photograph in character would sell at twice that figure. A signed cast photograph of all seven cast members sold for $750 at auction last year.

**"Lost in Space"** (From 1965-1968)—Our next pick is the hit sci-fi series "Lost In Space." Once again, a complete cast photograph is very rare, due to only one cast member, actor Guy Williams (who also played TV's "Zorro"). The only deceased cast member and a tough signer, his signature sells at $150. The other cast members have all done reunion and other nostalgia shows, generously signing photographs in character, that each sell for around $40. Even the man inside the robot, Bob May, sells signed photographs of himself, standing by the Robot, in the same price range. The other cast members include actress June Lockhart, Angela Cartwright, and Marta Kristen. Actors Mark Goddard, Bill Mumy, and Jonathan Harris round out the cast.

**"Star Trek"** (From 1966-1969)—Our eighth in the collectible casts is "Star Trek." An entire book could be written about the "Star Trek" crew and their individual signing habits in the past thirty years. Suffice to say, a cast-signed photograph sells at $550. There are many that were signed for an autograph firm and sold on a shopping channel in the last few years. There were several thousand in each edition. But we still recommend purchasing one, as all of the cast members are getting older, and the three main ones already have stopped signing. The original cast includes William Shatner, Leonard Nimoy, Deforest Kelley, Nichelle Nichols, James Doohan, Walter Koening, and George Takai.

**"All In The Family"** (From 1971-1981)—Another popular cast among collectors is this multiple Emmy award-winning cast and show. Interestingly, only the four principals are collected or considered a cast, but many neighbors and other characters appeared and spun off into their own successful series, including Bea Arthur in "Maude" and Isabel Sanford and Sherman Hemsley in "The Jeffersons." The main cast members were Sally Struthers, Rob Reiner, Carroll O'Connor, and Jean Stapleton. A cast photograph signed by all four currently sells for around $150.

**"M.A.S.H."** (From 1972-1983)—"M.A.S.H.'s" final episode is still the most watched TV event in history. Many cast members came and went over the years, but a few were constant. Alan Alda, who is a notoriously tough signer, played "Hawkeye Pierce." It doesn't matter that Alan Alda hasn't had a great career in films—he made up for it by starring for  over a decade on TV in the hit series "M.A.S.H." He is not a friendly signer, however, and authentic signatures are scarcer than you would think. Signatures sell for $25, and photographs ("M.A.S.H." images are the most collectible) sell for $50. A few documents have sold for $75. His swamp inhabitants were actors Wayne Rogers, Mike Farrell, and David Ogden Stiers. Rogers and Farrell routinely sign mail, with signed photographs in character selling at $40 a piece. Stiers will rarely sign M.A.S.H. material. McLean Stevenson, as the first "Colonel," is deceased and scarce, but the longer running "Colonel Potter" played by Harry Morgan is easier to obtain, as Morgan signs in person for fans and fan mail. His signed pictures as "Potter" sell for $40. Loretta Swit, who played "Hotlips," is an uncommon signer, selling at twice these other estimates. Jamie Farr, who gave us the hilarious "Corporal Klinger" signs fan mail and at shows, keeping his price on photographs reasonable in the $40 range. Bill Christopher still does many regional theatre acting roles, and signs as "Father Mucalhey" for fans, in the same price range. Gary Burghoff will also graciously sign fan mail as "Radar O'Reilly," and often sketches a self-caricature for fans. A cast photograph signed by all principal actors from a given season sells at $350 plus, currently.

**"Happy Days"** (From 1974-1984)—Debuting in 1974 and running for ten years, "Happy Days" made us all yearn for the good old days. Set in the 1950s, the show also spun off other hit shows, including "Mork and Mindy" and "Laverne and Shirley." The regular cast never changed until late in the series, when various actors were added to try to boost ratings. With the exception of "Al," who ran the drive-in and restaurant named "Als," the regular cast remained unchanged. Ron Howard played "Ritchie" and his sister, "Joanie," was played by Erin Moran. "Dad" was played by Tom Bosley and actress Marion Ross played "Mom Cunningham." The three friends were "Ralph," "Potsie," and the stand out, "Fonzie." They were played by Donny Most, Anson Williams, and Henry Winkler, respectively. Only Erin Moran is a tough signer, as she feels the show ruined her life—no doubt because her career ended when the show did. She sells for around $40 for a signature, although a few documents have sold in the $100 range. The remaining signatures sell for around $20 each, with a cast-signed photograph without Moran selling for around $200.

151

**"Saturday Night Live"** (From 1975-    )—Of all of the TV series in the past, no other single show has showcased and started as many careers as the show called "Saturday Night Live." The entire premise of the show was to constantly change its cast members year in and out, who would hone their skills live before a studio audience in weekly sketches of comedy. The show was the first to feature many new musical acts as well, including Bob Segar.

For many autograph fans, this is a fun cast to collect because it is always adding new members and has been on the air now for twenty two years! It first aired October 11, 1975, with an original cast that numbered nine in total. They attempted to bring fresh and outrageous comedy to late night viewers. Each show was ninety minutes long with a different guest host each week, who would also appear in sketches with the regular players, around whom many of the show's more memorable sketches were written.

Chevy Chase in the opening season made headlines by opening the show with a different pratfall. Chase also started the long running tradition of the news segment called "Weekend Update." The second year, Jane Curtin took over the news. Gilda Radner  gave incredible comic turns with such characters as "Barbara Wa Wa" (a send up of Barbara Walters; Walters hated it) and "RoseanRoseannaDanna." She married actor Gene Wilder and fought a brave fight against cancer that took her life in 1989. (She starred opposite her husband in several films such as *Hanky Panky* and *Haunted Honeymoon* shortly before her death.) John Belushi and Dan Aykroyd made music history when a sketch of theirs called the "Blues Brothers" paid homage to real life singers "Sam and Dave" and spawned a number one hit, an album, and even a hit movie of the same name.

Many original short films were aired over the years, starting with Jim Henson's "Muppets," followed by Albert Brooks film shorts. More memorable were the "Mr. Bill" film shorts in clay. Chevy Chase was the first to hit film stardom, followed quickly by Belushi and Aykroyd. Later, Eddie Murphy hit superstardom after appearing on the show. In later years, Billy Crystal, Jon Lovitz, David Spade, Chris Farley, Martin Short, Dennis Miller, Dana Carvey, and Mike Myers also left for larger screen careers.

The original nine cast members were: Chevy Chase, John Belushi, Dan Aykroyd, Gilda Radner, Garrett Morris, Jane Curtin, Laraine Newman, Albert Brooks, and Jim Henson's Muppets. In 1976, the cast remained relatively unchanged from their first year, adding only Gary Weis to the stellar lineup of what the show promoted as the "Not Ready for Prime Time Players." Bill Murray was added in 1977. In 1978, Don Novello and Paul Shaffer joined the band. In 1979, Al Franken and Tom Davis joined as writers and sometime players.

In 1980, Gilbert Gottfried, Joe Piscopo, and Charles Rocket joined the cast. It would be Bill Murray's last year, as he started appearing in films like *Caddyshack*. Newman, Morris, and Radner would all leave in 1980 as well. Akyroyd and Belushi left at the start of the year. Chevy Chase was only on board that first year.

In 1981, Eddie Murphy, Tony Rosato, Christine Ebersole, Brian Doyle Murray (Bill's older brother), and Mary Gross were added to fill the vacating actors' shoes. In 1982, Brad Hall took over their mock news segment and Julia Louis Dreyfus (later of "Seinfeld") was added.

In 1983, Jim Belushi (John's brother) was added. In 1984, the cast expanded to include: Billy Crystal, Christopher Guest, Harry Shearer, Rich Hall, and Martin Short, in a major cast overhaul. In 1985, Anthony Michael Hall, Randy Quaid, Joan Cusack, Nora Dunn, Terry Sweeney, Jon Lovitz, Damon Wayans, and Robert Downey revamped the cast. Years later, Damon and his brothers would launch a similiarly formatted show called "In Living Color," which would showcase talent like Jim Carrey.

In 1986, Dennis Miller took over the news segment and Phil Hartman, Dana Carvey, Jan Hooks, Victoria Jackson, and Kevin Nealon were added. In 1987 and 1988, no changes were made. In 1989, Mike Myers was added. In 1990, Chris Farley, Chris Rock, and Julia Sweeney were added. In 1991, Ellen Claghorne, Tim Meadows, Adam Sandler, Rob Schneider, and David Spade were added to the cast.

As with any cast that is this large in collecting scope, there are easy ones and tougher ones to acquire. Tragically, we have already lost several of the cast members. John Belushi died of a drug overdose in 1983, followed by Gilda Radner, who passed away after a long battle with cancer. Chris Farley was found dead in his apartment at age 33. Not surprisingly, these are also the three key signatures to obtain, and also the three priciest.

John Belushi was a tough signer. His signature sells for around $200 when encountered. A few (approx. 40) checks signed by him were sold at auction by his wife Judy Jacklin, and these sell around $500 each at present. Signed photographs, mainly of The Blues Brothers, sell at around $400. Gilda Radner lived longer and signed a lot more for fans. Her signature is rising in value, however, currently selling around $90. A few documents signed by her have surfaced selling in the $200 range, as do signed photographs. Chris Farley was a friendly signer, but his death has caught most dealers flat-footed. The market has not had time to set his price, but he has already sold at $50 for a signature, and $125 on a photograph. The remaining cast members sell each in the $10-30 range for single signatures, and roughly twice that on their respective photographs. The bigger stars are obviously the tougher to obtain, as the demands on their time are greater.

Authentic examples of many of the cast members have been shown for your authenticating purposes. Time will tell in the modern show lineups which will be considered a classic in years to come, but here are a few of the more recent shows that are heavily collected today based on demand from dealers.

**"Cheers"** (From 1982-1993)—The show is well loved by many fans. There was not much of a cast change over the years, with two exceptions. Nick Colosanto, who played "Coach," died after the shows' first three years. He is a fairly scarce signature valued at $100 and up. Kirstie Alley replaced Shelly Long midway through the series, and Bebe Neuwrith joined the show as the psychiatrist wife of Kelsey Grammer's character "Dr. Frasier Crane," who spun off into his own hot TV show. The rest of the regulars included: Rhea Perlman, Ted Dansen, Woody Harrelson, George Wendt, and John Ratzenberger. Cast photographs signed by all (except Colasanto) with one or the other female leads (Long or Alley) sell for around $300 on a photograph, or you can assemble them all for around $25 each.

# ROCK AND ROLL HALL OF FAME

For those of us who cannot afford to collect a set of the Signers of the Declaration of Independence, or an example of each of the U.S. Presidents, the Rock and Roll Hall of Fame represents a fun and profitable collection that is still obtainable without mortgaging the family home.

It's hard to believe it took until the 1980s to form a Rock and Roll Hall of Fame, and thereafter, a museum with the same name in Cleveland, Ohio. Every year the Hall of Fame committee inducts new members into their hallowed hall that includes writers, singers, and musicians who have shaped rock and roll music since its inception in the 1950s. The first inductions were announced in 1986, and have continued yearly ever since. This is a complete list, with signing habits where appropriate, and pricing information on the artists that have been inducted each year.

It is fun to collect Hall of Fame members. Many collectors like collecting categories that include a finite number of people —such as all the artists who have won a Tony (Broadway), Emmy (TV) or Oscar (Film) award, just as sports lovers collect Baseball and other Sports Hall of Famers. One of the newest hot collections going is that of the members of the Rock and Roll Hall of Fame.

As Ed Sullivan might have said, "Tonight, we've got a really big 'shoe' for you people . . . and here they are . . ."

**Chuck Berry** (1926-    )—Born Charles Edward Anderson Berry, Chuck Berry's innovations to the fledgling field of rock and roll music can be felt in the decades of rock music since in the vocals, style, and guitar work of nearly every band that followed him. It was blues legend Muddy Waters who suggested  that Berry should record a demo tape and send it to the head of Chess Records in 1955; and when he did, "Maybellene" became his first hit that same year. Scores of classics followed, like "Johnny B. Goode" and "Roll Over Beethoven." Berry has never signed fan mail and it is doubtful he ever will. He is equally tough to get to sign in person; therefore, his signatures sell at around $50, with signed photographs and album covers hitting $100 or more. He has signed the occasional guitar, which brings $1200 plus at auction, but none of his personal guitars have sold privately. In fact, his famed crimson-colored guitar he named "Lucille" will be given to the Smithsonian at his death. For years when he did sign, it would be in full like the one shown here, signed in 1964. In later years he has often signed just "C. Berry," sometimes adding a smiley face drawing.
**Scarcity Index—★★**

**James Brown** (1933-    )—Probably the most influential of the early African American singers, his style is evident in Black music to this day. His most memorable hits like "Papa's Got a Brand New Bag" and "I Feel Good" are still a staple of radio airplay. A friendly signer, he is worthy of the nickname "Godfather of Soul." A signature can be had for around $25, with a signed photograph at around $50. Personal hardships aside, he is deserved of the title "Hardest Working Man in Show Business," with a career spanning forty years and counting.
**Scarcity Index—★★**

**Ray Charles** (1930-    )—Contrary to what you may think, Ray Charles has signed for fans, most notably in the presence of managers he trusts to tell him what was put before him to sign! He signs because he can; he lost his sight at the age of seven, but had learned to write. He went on to master the piano in his teens, and soon was writing scores of songs. Among his early hits is the R&B classic "I've Got a Woman." Later, in the 1960s, he went more pop mainstream with hits like "Hit the Road Jack" and his signature song, "Georgia on My Mind." (He was from Macon, Georgia.) His signing is still scarce, though, with a few documents hitting the market at $300, and signed photographs at $150. Signatures alone sell at about $65.
**Scarcity Index—★★★**

**Sam Cooke** (1931-1964)—Cooke began in music as a successful religious singer with his unusual tenor style putting him as the lead singer in several groups. It was his second career into secular (pop) music that made him famous worldwide with the release of his first hit "You Send Me," in 1957. In the years 1962 and 1963 he had nine consecutive R&B Top Ten hits: songs like "Another Saturday Night" and "Twisting the Night Away." His untimely death at the height of his career in December 1964 is partly responsible for his high value, with signatures selling near $300, and signed photographs at over twice that figure.
**Scarcity Index—★★★★**

**Fats Domino** (1928-    )—Domino sold more records in the 1950s than any other Black artist. His boogie woogie piano-pounding style set the tone through almost 40 Top Ten hits like "Ain't That a Shame" and "Blueberry Hill." He has signed fan mail off and on for years, enough to keep his prices low, at around $15 for a signature, and $35 on a photograph. Signed copies of lyrics to songs like "Blueberry Hill" show up around $60 from time to time, as well.
**Scarcity Index—★**

**The Everly Brothers** (Formed 1956)—The real life brothers, Don and Phil, set the tone for two-part harmonies that later groups like the Beatles, the Hollies, Simon and Garfunkel, and others emulated. Their first song release, "Bye Bye Love," was a hit, and they would enjoy three years of consecutive hits thereafter, such as "Wake Up Little Susie" and "All I Have to Do Is Dream." But in the 1960s their personal lives were shattered with a series of events. Both were drafted into the Army; Don became addicted to "Speed," which nearly killed him; and they tired of working together professionally. Apart, they never regained what they shared together. They are both friendly signers, which has kept the price of their material reasonable. Signatures of the two sell at $40, with signed photographs and albums at $80.
**Scarcity Index—★★**

**Buddy Holly** (1936-1959)—Born Charles Hardin Holley in Texas, he started performing Country & Western like so many of the early rock pioneers. After a chance meeting with Elvis Presley, he added R&B to his act and formed the group, the Crickets, during which time he scored his first big hit "That'll Be the Day," in 1957. The next year he experimented with many recording techniques, like echo effects, to score big with "Peggy Sue" and "Maybe Baby," among others. Shortly after marrying, and after only 18 months of fame, he left on the Winter Dance Tour that would claim his life and those of the Big Bopper and Ritchie Valens, when their plane crashed on February 3, 1959. He was a friendly signer, but had little time to sign before his death. If it were not for the many things sold years later at auction by his family, he may have remained extremely rare. Still scarce, they sold many greeting cards he had signed to family members, and homework of which even the unsigned pages, properly documented from the family's sale, bring $400 today. Signatures bring as much, with rarer signed photographs bringing $1000 and up. Very few documents have surfaced.
**Scarcity Index—★★★★**

**Jerry Lee Lewis** (1935-  )—The last of the 1950s wild stars in concert—and in private—"The Killer," as he nicknamed himself, was a child genius on piano, as were his cousins, the Reverend Jimmy Swaggert and country star and nightclub owner Mickey Gilley. He might have been dubbed the "King of Rock and Roll" instead of Elvis had he not married his 13-year-old cousin in 1958, a scandal that caused his career to come to a halt. He never fully recovered from the setback, career-wise. His boogie woogie piano classics like "Great Balls of Fire" will always be remembered, though. He has signed fan mail in the past and done signings for autograph firms, keeping his signature reasonable at around $20, and photographs at $50. Many early letters and documents have hit the market recently, selling anywhere from $200 and up, depending on content and historical importance to his career.

**Scarcity Index—★**

**Elvis Presley** (1935-1977)—An entire book could be written on the "King of Rock and Roll." Doubtful we need remind you of his influence on rock, his personality, song, and movie titles—all considerable. His untimely death has made his signature continue to soar in value, although he signed for a great many people. A signature sells currently at around $500, with signed photographs at around $900. Several auctions of his cars, stage jumpsuits, and even personal effects like his American Express credit card, have all netted millions of dollars. Scarcity isn't the issue as much as how much you can afford to spend on a nice collectible. Letters exist, although they were normally typed by a secretary and signed by him later. Handwritten letters and documents start at around $1500 and up in price.

**Scarcity Index—★★★**

**Little Richard** (1935-    )—His flamboyant stage style is still imitated today by artists such as Prince. He is a brilliant piano player and a good businessman, who far before anyone else in music history, retained the rights to his songs. Later in life he became an ordained minister, even officiating at the marriage of Demi Moore and actor Bruce Willis. He is not a friendly signer, and was reclusive for years, but recently signed a contract with an autograph firm, signing posters and 8 x 10 photographs, which sell for $65 and $125, respectively. (Until these are all sold, and he starts signing again, they are the market prices.) Scarcity is currently not an issue. With pioneering style in hits like "Good Golly Miss Molly" and "Tutti Fruitti," he will always be collected. A few documents have hit the market in the $250 range, signed with his real name, "Richard Penniman." **Scarcity Index—★★★**

**In 1987, fifteen performers were inducted into the Hall of Fame instead of the 10 from the first year, as the committee was still playing catch-up. These inductees were:**

**The Coaster**s (Formed 1955)—One of the original of the "Doo Wop" groups, with a string of whimsical hits. The group originally consisted of two men: Carl Gardner, who was the lead vocalist, and Bobby Nunn, who sang with him. Although literally dozens of other groups have used the name over the years, performing in old 1950s reunion shows, these were the originals who were inducted into the hall of Fame. Prices not available from this past year.
**Scarcity Index—Original Coasters—★★★★**

**Eddie Cochrane** (1938-1960)—Cochrane had a lot in common with Buddy Holly. They were friends, they both were songwriters, in addition to singers, and both did innovative things while recording, such as overdubbing. They had one more thing in common: both died tragically as their careers were just starting. On a London tour in 1960, after the release of his first big hit "Summertime Blues," Eddie was killed in a car crash. He was only 21. Years later, "Summertime Blues" would be the group The Who's biggest hit as well. Because of these circumstances, material signed by him is very rare. We had no examples last year to cite for price, although a year earlier a signature sold for $400.
**Scarcity Index—★★★★★**

**Bo Diddly** (1928-   )—Born Ella Otha Bates McDaniels (you would go by a nickname like "Bo," too, wouldn't you?) His beat and guitar and vocal style had deep African roots. His 1950s and 1960s style influenced far into the future, reaching even the Rap music genre of today. His most memorable hit was "Who Do You Love," but he had several others. He has always been a gracious signer when approached after a gig, like in a blues club, where he still performs today. A signature is worth $20, and a photograph is worth $50.
**Scarcity Index—★★**

**Aretha Franklin** (1942-   )—Called by fans the "Queen of Soul" or "Lady Soul," she had a long string of hits for over seven years, with the most memorable being "Respect." Even 25 years later she was topping the charts opposite pop star George Michael, in a duet. She has always been a friendly signer, keeping her signature affordable at $25 and signed photographs at $50. A couple of documents for concert appearances have sold lately in the $150 range.
**Scarcity Index—★★**

**Marvin Gaye** (1939-1984)—One of Motown's early recording artists (he married Motown founder Barry Gordy's sister, Anna Gordy), he consistently stayed at the top of the charts in the 1960s and 1970s. He hit number one a few times with songs like "I Heard it Through the Grapevine" and "How Sweet It Is to Be Loved By You." He loved duets and had many hits with Mary Wells and Kim Preston, but he really hit his stride dueting with Tammi Terrell in hits like "Ain't Nothing Like the Real Thing Baby." He was devastated when she died of a brain tumor in 1970. He became reclusive for a while, and encountered a long string of personal and business problems, including back tax disputes with the IRS and a nasty divorce from Anna. He fled to Europe, where he stayed for years, returning with a number one hit in 1982, "Sexual Healing," only to be shot to death in 1984 by his minister father during an argument. He is fairly scarce in material for the above reasons. A few checks and documents have sold around $350, and signed photographs will bring $300.
**Scarcity Index—★★★★**

**Bill Haley** (1927-1981)—DJ Arthur Freed may have coined the phrase "rock and roll," but Bill Haley first used it in the hit song, "Rock Around the Clock." He had started in country music, and had been the leader of several bands, but in early rock with the Comets he would enjoy the most fame. After "Rock Around the Clock" he scored nine more hits, including "See You Later Alligator." He was a tough signer, and due to his place in rock history, is in great demand for collectors, with signed photographs selling at $700 plus, and signatures at $400. Documents are scarcer.
**Scarcity Index—★★★★**

**B.B. King** (1925-   )—Riley B. "Blues Boy" King, one of the most influential guitarists ever, invented his own blues guitar, "the vibrator," which is still used by blues musicians to this day. He has won every major music award, and performed for political leaders and royalty the world over. After over forty years in music, he still performed over 130 club dates last year, after which he is usually very gracious to autograph collectors. His signature sells at $20, with signed photographs at $50.
**Scarcity Index—★★**

**Clyde McPhatter** (1932-1972)—Along with Ray Charles, Clyde McPhatter was an innovative force in early 1950s vocals. He formed two groups, the Dominoes and the Drifters, around his lead singing style, and had solo hits as well, but many personal problems caused him to fade into obscurity before passing away in 1972. He was an extremely rare signer, with the last recorded sale of a signature being for $500 a few years ago. Other forms, such as documents and photographs, are even rarer.
**Scarcity Index—★★★★★**

**Ricky Nelson** (1940-1985)—The son of the popular radio and later TV clan, the Nelsons. Little Ricky became a teen heartthrob at age 16 with his rendition of "I'm Walkin." At age 21, he dropped the "y" in his name to show he had matured, but as Rick Nelson had only one hit in 1972 with "Garden Party." He was doing a reunion tour when he died in 1985, in a plane crash. He was always a friendly signer for fans, and a few documents have surfaced as well. The documents have sold in the $200-250 range, with signatures at $125, and signed photographs at around $200.
**Scarcity Index—★★★**

**Roy Orbison** (1936-1988)—With his unusual tenor voice and grumbling trademark growls, who can forget any of Orbison's early hits like "Pretty Woman" or "Crying?" After a thirty year career, he was hitting the charts again with a distinguished group of peers in the Travelling Willburys at the time of his death from a heart attack. Always a friendly signer, his signature is fairly uncommon and sells at $125, with signed photographs at $300. He never signed fan mail.
**Scarcity Index—★★★**

**Carl Perkins** (1932-1998)—The history of rock and roll could not be told without mentioning Carl Perkins. According to Eric Clapton and George Harrison, he taught them to play and he wrote many of Johnny Cash's hits. His own hit "Blue Suede Shoes" would be number one on three charts, and a later monster hit for Elvis Presley. He played clubs and fairs, touring every year, and was a gracious signer, showing his roots in country western music. He signed his fan mail sporadically, and even did a limited handwritten edition of his lyrics for "Blue Suede Shoes" for an autograph company. The handwritten lyrics were available for several hundred dollars, but his signature is common at around $15, with signed photographs and some letters selling for around $40.
**Scarcity Index—★**

**Smokey Robinson** (1940-   )—One of the most prolific song writers of all time, especially for Motown (over 1500 songs published). He wrote for Diana Ross, Martha and the Vandellas, and his own mega group, the Miracles. Covering his songs years later launched careers for Linda Ronstadt and the Captain and Tenneille, with Robinson hits like "Muskrat Love" and "Shop Around." A few documents have hit the market in the $150 range and his signature can be had for around $30, with signed photographs selling at around $55. He signs in person, and has signed fan mail off and on for years.
**Scarcity Index—★★**

**Big Joe Turner** (1911-1985)—In the 1950s, a string of hits brought the R&B artist pop preeminence. Songs like "Shake, Rattle and Roll" and "Hush Honey" would be bigger hits for other artists later, but he was their originator, with a unique sound many later emulated. He died in 1985, and was always a bit reclusive, and perhaps not approached as he should have been for his autograph, making it quite scarce today. No recorded sales this past year to give as a marker for price.
Scarcity Index—★★★★★

**Muddy Waters** (1915-1983)—Known for working his audiences up like Jerry Lee Lewis would later do, Muddy Waters had an urgent style to his vocals and blues that was unique Delta Louisiana styling. Eric Clapton, Johnny Winter, and others performed with him, and the Rolling Stones named themselves after his hit "Rollin Stone." He became known as the "Father of the Electric Blues." He was always a scarce signer, with his signature, now that he is deceased, selling at around $200, and signed photographs selling at $400 or more.
Scarcity Index—★★★★

**Jackie Wilson** (1934-1984)- No one could deny the vocal prowess of Jackie Wilson. He started with the Dominoes, but as a solo artist had his biggest hits like "Lonely Teardrops" and "Higher and Higher." He collapsed on stage in 1975 and entered a coma, which lasted for 8 and a half years, before he passed away. He was a tough signer, and is quite rare today, with signatures selling for $300, and photographs being quite rare. A few documents have sold in the $400 range, as well.
Scarcity Index—★★★★

**In 1988, the Hall of Fame committee realized they needed to start selecting carefully and slow their pacing down so as to not run out of inductees soon. For this reason they decided to induct only 5 artists. They included:**

**The Beach Boys** (Formed 1950s)—The core of the original group was three brothers: Brian, Carl, and Dennis Wilson. They added a cousin, Al Jardine, and a best friend, Mike Love, and became The Beach Boys. They had a unique style dubbed "surf music," with songs about school and cars and girls and the beach. After several hits, citing fatigue, Brian Wilson left from performing with them and only wrote songs and produced. The group added Bruce Johnston to replace Wilson onstage, and had even more hits like "Help Me Rhonda"and "I Get Around." After many personal problems, including drug addiction, Brian left the group entirely. In 1983, Dennis Wilson died in a drowning accident. This served to reinvigorate the group, which produced a hit song for the film *Cocktail* called "Kokomo." The group has not performed together since 1992. Several nice documents signed by the original members of the group have sold in the $500-600 range. Signed vintage photographs of the original group sell for around $450, with signatures alone bringing around $250.
**Scarcity Index—★★★**

**The Beatles** (Formed 1959)—The Fab Four could fill a book by themselves. Landing on American shores in 1964, they have influenced pop music ever since. Let's run down signing habits, instead of their life histories, which every Beatles fan knows. When the Beatles were at their height, many people met them at concerts and other events and believed that when they sent their autograph books backstage, they would be getting authentic autographs. However, it is now well-known that their touring manager, Neil Aspinall, often handled signing for them. There are authentic examples from the 1960s, however, and a page signed by all four will cost around $1800 today. If the four signatures are spread out across more than one page, a set would run about $1300. A signed photograph from this time period will run at least $3000, but watch out again for printed fan club signatures or secretarials. Individual signatures break down this way: John Lennon—$600 (deceased); Paul McCartney—$250; George Harrison—$200; Ringo Starr—$150. Documents signed by all four are rare, with the last two at auction selling for $7500 and $10,000, respectively. Business checks have surfaced on Ringo Starr, John Lennon, and George Harrison, currently selling at $300, $1400, and $700, respectively. Paul McCartney checks are very rare. Would you like to own handwritten lyrics from a classic Beatles song? Better get a bank loan. They have sold at auction from $40,000 to $250,000!

**Scarcity Index—(All Four)** ★★★★
**John—★★★★ Paul—★★★**
**George—★★★ Ringo—★★**

**The Drifters** (Formed 1953)—The original group's lead singer was Clyde McPhatter, and later Ben E. King, among others. Although the roster of talent constantly changed, they would rule the charts with hits for twelve years. Their romantic styling would produce hits like "Up on the Roof" and "Under the Boardwalk." The current group has none of the original members, and tours retro-oldies scenes. The originals included Rudy Lewis and Johnny Moore, in addition to McPhatter. No price can be established for a piece signed by McPhatter or the rest, such is the scarcity. The best bet would be to assemble the group's individual signatures.
Scarcity Index—★★★★★

**Bob Dylan** (1941-  )—Poet Laureate to a nation, Dylan's son is now enjoying chart success. His antiwar anthems ignited a country ready to hear them. He has performed before presidents and the Pope. He is a notorious non-signer, to such a degree that he is the most expensive signature of all the living artists, with signatures selling for $200, and photographs selling at $500. A few documents have sold in the $750 range. He is likely to stay a tough signer who will only rise in value after his death.
**Scarcity Index—★★★★**

**The Supremes** (Formed 1959)—Diana Ross and the Supremes were probably Motown's biggest hit makers. Although Diana broke up the group to go on to solo success, vintage material signed by her and the Supremes is scarce. Their harmonies produced a string of great hits, culminating in the farewell song "Someday We'll Be Together." Diana is a fairly nice signer, selling for around $50 on photographs today, but material signed by her and the original Supremes is quite scarce. Her original background Supremes were singers Mary Wells and Florence Ballard, but Ballard was replaced in 1967 by singer Cindy Birdsong. Ballard would die penniless in 1976. The original Supremes, with the exception of Wells, are the scarcer of the trios to obtain, but it can be done. Contracts signed by them all have sold for $600 plus, while a vintage set of signatures would be worth around $250.

**Scarcity Index—★★★★**

**In 1989, the committee continued inducting artists somewhat sparingly as they had in 1988, with the artists inducted including:**

**Dion** (1939-   )—Born Dion DiMucci, his soulful vocal style stood out against a backdrop of doo wop groups in the 1950s. He originally fronted for a group called Dion and the Belmonts, and had several hits like "A Teenager in Love" with them, but they parted company in 1960 and his solo career would churn out eight more top ten hits like "Runaround Sue" and "The Wanderer." He was always a friendly signer, even signing fan mail off and on for years. His signature sells for $30, with a signed photograph or album jacket around $60.
**Scarcity Index—★★**

**Otis Redding** (1941-1967)—One of only three artists to have a hit posthumously. This hit was "Sittin on the Dock of the Bay." He died in a plane crash in December 1967. His signature is quite scarce, with the last one recorded two years ago selling for $300. Other signed material is even rarer.
**Scarcity Index—★★★★★**

**The Rolling Stones** (Formed 1963)—Everyone over the age of ten knows at least one hit by this group which is still selling out arenas today, so we will concentrate on their signing habits and group members for now. The original group included Mick Jagger, Keith Richards, Dick Taylor, and Mick Avery. Richards and Jagger had been classmates. After their first public appearance, they replaced Avery and Taylor with drummer Charlie Watts and bassist Bill Wyman, and brought in Brian Jones. These were the classic original Stones who churned out dozens of hits like "I Can't Get No Satisfaction" and "Jumpin Jack Flash." In 1969, they fired Brian Jones, who died shortly afterwards. They replaced his vacancy with Ron Wood. The original group goes for $1000 on a signed photograph, with the new lineup selling at around $550. Very few documents have surfaced as of this writing. Individual signed photographs of Richards and Jagger sell for around $100 each.
**Scarcity Index— Original Lineup— ★★★★★**
**Current Stones— ★★★**

**The Temptations** (Formed 1961)—The Temptations emerged from Motown at the same time as the Supremes. Smokey Robinson wrote some of their biggest hits like "The Way You Do The Things You Do" and "My Girl." The original lineup was David Ruffin and Eddie Kendricks, with various session players as backup vocals. Ruffin left the group in 1968 and Kendricks left in 1971. Afterwards, like the Drifters and Coasters, there have been many other "Temptations" touring and singing the old songs; but without Ruffin or Kendricks, their reign at the top of the charts was over. The original two on photographs sell at around $150. Documents have not yet surfaced.
**Scarcity Index—★★★**

**Stevie Wonder** (1950-    )—Unlike Ray Charles, Stevie Wonder was always blind and has never learned to write his name. Even documents that have surfaced are "signed" by applying his thumbprint to the document. Even a "signed" photograph to long time friend Sammy Davis, Jr. was a thumbprint, so any reportedly signed photographs are forgeries and should be avoided like the plague. The documents that have surfaced sell in the $200-$300 range. His first hit "Fingertips" was at Motown when he was only a teen. In the thirty years since, he has turned out many classics like "Signed, Sealed, Delivered" and "My Cherie Amour."
**Scarcity Index—Documents Only ★★★**

**In 1990, twice as many artists were inducted than the year before including:**

**Louis Armstrong** (1900-1971)—The gravel-voiced "Great Satchmo" appeared in films like *Hello Dolly* portraying himself. An accomplished jazz singer and trumpeter, he is highly collected today. A few signed 78 rpm records have traded hands in the last few years, as has an odd document or two. His signature and signed photographs both maintain good value today at $200 and $500, respectively. Even more desirable, he often signed his nickname "Satchmo," in addition to his signature, on photographs and album books of fans. A signed record sold for $600 recently and a document sold at auction for $500.
Scarcity Index—★★★

**Hank Ballard** (1936-    )—Influential more than a hitmaker, Ballard performed with the Royals, and later the Midnighters, before a string of solo successes. He is a scarce signature on any material, with no documented sales in the last year from which to report a value.
Scarcity Index—★★★★

**Bobby Darin** (1936-1973)—As a folk singer in the 1960s or a Sinatra-style crooner in the 1950s— or even as a rocker— Darin did it all, and left a wake of hits in all three styles. He was always a great signer, even signing his fan mail from time to time. His signature is currently at $20, with a signed photograph at around $45.
Scarcity Index—★

**The Four Seasons** (Formed 1962)—The original group consisted of guitarist Tommy Devito, writer and vocalist Bob Gaudio, and lead singer Frankie Valli. The almost unreal falsetto voice of Valli makes their songs immediately recognizable from the rest of the groups of their era. Early in their hit making career—ten top-ten hits between 1963 and 1967—they were thought by many to be Black performers, and had a large R&B following with hits like "Sherry" and "Big Girls Don't Cry." But, with their popularity waning by 1967, Valli left the group for a solo career. He had many solo hits including "My Eyes Adored You," but the Seasons, as they now called themselves, never hit the charts again. Valli has always been a friendly signer, with signed material selling at $25-50 on photographs, depending on whether or not other band members are included as well.
**Scarcity Index—★**

**The Four Tops** (Formed 1954)—Unlike the Temptations and other multi-member acts, the Four Tops never changed band members. The four—Levi Stubbs Jr. (lead vocal), Lawrence Payton, Abdul Fakir, and Renaldo Benson—met in high school, and had their first hit when Motown signed them in 1963 with the song "Baby, I Need Your Lovin." They had years of hits afterwards, like "Reach Out and I'll Be There" and "I Can't Help Myself." Although they have not scored a hit since 1981, they still tour and perform the old standards together. When you can approach them, they are willing signers. A set of signatures sells for approximately $60, with a photograph signed by all four in the $100 range. A few vintage documents have sold in the $200 range, as well.
**Scarcity Index—★★**

**The Kinks** (Formed 1964)—Major shuffling of band members over the years make this band tough to collect. For the purist, the original lineup of 1960s rockers were two brothers, Ray and Dave Davies, who brought in two classmates, Peter Quaife and drummer Mick Avory. "You Really Got Me" was the group's first smash hit. Legal suits kept the band from touring America, however, which hurt their momentum for five years. John Gosling was added to the band when they recorded their next smash, and finally toured the U.S. with the hit song "Lola." Quaiff left the band in 1968 and John Dalton came on. Dalton came and went twice more. Andy Pyle came and went. Gosling left. Three others joined. Two left. You get the picture. No other major hits happened until "Come Dancing" in 1982. The band has had no hits since then. For collecting purposes, a band photograph or signed album needs to have Ray Davies (lead singer) and brother Dave, who were the only founders and longtime members. Photographs signed with these combinations sell around $150 each.
**Scarcity Index—★★★★**

**The Platters** (Formed 1953)—With tenor Tony Williams on lead vocals, the Platters charted an incredible thirty-five Top 100 hits in the 1950s and 1960s. Classics like "Only You," "The Great Pretender," and "Smoke Gets in Your Eyes" tore up the radio waves. The background members changed off and on, and Williams is the only must-have signature. His signature on a card is valued at $50-60, with a group photograph at $100-150.
**Scarcity Index—★★★**

**Simon and Garfunkel** (Formed 1957)—Paul Simon has had a folksy kind of career with a handful of hits after breaking up with longtime partner Art Garfunkel. Art has not had any big hits as a solo artist and now sticks mainly to writing and producing, but together, they were chart magic. In the 1960s they dueted on such classics as "Bridge Over Troubled Waters" and "Cecilia" before breaking up to go in different artistic directions. In the 1980s, they reunited for a standing room only crowd in New York's Central Park. Apart from one another they both are friendly signers, and since both maintain residences in New York City, it is tough but not impossible to run into both of them. A signed photograph or album of the two sells at around $150, with signatures alone at about $60.
Scarcity Index—★★

**The Who** (Formed 1964)—Founded by Pete Townsend along with John Entwistle and Roger Daltry, the Who was a major part of the British Invasion of the 1960s. Their first hit came with the band's innovative sound on "My Generation," but worldwide success swallowed them with their rock opera *Tommy*. When they started to tour, drummer Keith Moon joined the band. Moon died in 1978 and Pete Townsend had progressive hearing loss, making any other hits unlikely, so the band retired, coming back for a few "farewell" tours in the 1980s. They are fairly tough signers and Keith Moon, in particular, is always rare. A few documents and checks signed by Moon have surfaced, selling for around $250. A Moon signature alone is worth $100. The original with Moon on a photograph would be worth around $750 today, but more often you get a chance to purchase the original three that are still alive today: Daltry, Entwhistle, and Townsend. None of them live in the United States, making it a bit tougher, nor do they answer much fan mail, keeping even the threesome's price fairly respectable at around $300 on photographs.
Scarcity Index—w/Moon ★★★★★  The Three★★★

**In 1991, the committee selected the following new inductees:**

**Laverne Baker** (1929-1997)—A versatile blues singer, Baker scored over twenty R&B hits in the ten year period from 1955-1965. She even released a live album of her nightclub act in 1991. She still tours blues clubs and is a friendly signer for fans, with signatures running $20 and signed photographs at $40.
Scarcity Index—★★

**The Byrds** (Formed 1964)—Many believe this is the British Invasion group most responsible for the folk-rock style still felt today in much of popular music. The group originally consisted of Roger McGuinn, David Crosby, Gene Clark, and Michael Clark. Early hits were the classics, starting with the number one smash "Mr. Tambourine Man" and later a second number one with "Turn, Turn, Turn." Gene Clark, who wrote the songs for the group, left in late 1966, as did the lead vocalist, McGuinn. Late in 1968, they returned to to stage a comeback, but had only mildly successful hits thereafter. By the early 1970s, they had gone their separate ways. Only a few months after the band's 1991 Hall of Fame induction, Gene Clark died. In 1993, Michael Clark died. Vintage material signed by the band is rare with no photographs selling in the past year to quote. However, a few vintage documents signed by the band have sold in the $600 range. The two surviving members have little autograph value.
Scarcity Index—★★★★★

**John Lee Hooker** (1920-    )—John Lee Hooker stands apart as a creative blues original. From the 1940s to the present day, recording blues for every major and minor label in existence, he is a standard on the scene, often emulated, but never copied completely. He is a tough signer, and even though a legend, his signature is inexplicably scarce. Signatures can run $50-60, with signed photographs topping out at over $100.
Scarcity Index—★★★

**Wilson Pickett** (1941-    )—Dubbed "Wicked Pickett" by fans, his first hit was 1964's "In the Midnight Hour," but there would come many more such as "Land of a 1,000 Dances" and "Mustang Sally." A king of both dance music and slow romantic ballads, he has always been a friendly signer, with signed photographs selling at $45, and signatures at $20.
**Scarcity Index—★★**

**Jimmy Reed** (1925-1976)—Known for his harmonica solos as well as his unique vocal style, Reed crossed onto the pop charts more times than any other strictly blues artist, with hits like "Bright Lights, Big City" and "Going to New York." He has always been a gracious signer, with signatures selling at $20, and signed photographs at $40. He has on occasion signed fan mail as well.
**Scarcity Index—★★**

**Ike and Tina Turner** (Formed 1961)—Not on the best of terms today, the former husband and wife team must be obtained separately on albums and photographs, but both are willing signers. Ike still tours small clubs and shows, although he never again had the success the two had while together with such classics as "Proud Mary." A solo career was an easy transition for Tina, though, who has had hit after hit for over twenty-five years, with no sign of slowing down. She is the tougher signer only because she lives abroad and must be gotten after American talk show appearances, parties, charity events, or her own tours. Tina alone on a signed photograph is worth $50, with signatures at around $25. Ike sells in the same range. Signatures together are approximately double that figure, but if the two signed a piece during the 1960s while they were still together, it would sell for more as a vintage item. A couple of vintage documents signed by both have sold in the $250-300 range recently.
**Scarcity Index—On vintage items ★★★★**
**Modern signed items★★**

**In 1992, the Hall of Fame continued to induct just seven members, as they had the previous two years, with new inductees being:**

**Bobby "Blue" Bland** (1930-   )—Blues hits have poured forth from his distinctive pipes from 1953 to his last hit in the late 1980s, "Members Only." He is a bit reclusive after performances and a tough signer, but there is still time to get this blues legend. No prices existed in the last calendar year for a Bland piece to compare for a pricing.
**Scarcity Index—★★★★**

**Booker T and the MG's** (Formed 1963)—A top house band known for their instrumental hits more than vocal talents, the original band consisted of Booker T. Jones and Steve Cropper, who added Bassist Lewis Steinberg and drummer Al Jackson to round out the band. In a four year period in the late 1960s, they had several instrumental hits like "Green Onions" and "Hang Em High." By 1971, they broke up to pursue other projects, and in 1975, Al Jackson was shot and killed by a burglar in his home. In the late 1970s, Donald Dunn, who had replaced Steinberg and Cropper, worked with Dan Akyroyd and John Belushi's band the Blues Brothers. Vintage material signed by all, including Jackson, is quite scarce with no pricing from the past year to report. Signed photographs of Cropper, Dunn, and Booker T. Jones can be found.
**Scarcity Index—All Vintage★★★★★**
**Remaining members ★★★**

**Johnny Cash** (1932-    )—The only performer to be inducted into all three of music's Hall of Fames: The Rock and Roll Hall of Fame, The Country Music Hall of Fame, and the Songwriters Hall of Fame. From "I Walk the Line" to "Folsom Prison Blues," he has become as American as apple pie. Until he retired from touring recently, announcing to the world that he has Parkinson's Disease, he was the friendliest signer in all of music. He has also signed fan mail, and is under contract for a few different autograph dealers. In short, at around $30 for a signed photograph, we rate him as the best buy in autographs currently. You should walk—no, run—and get one in your collection before we lose this legend and the price shoots up.
**Scarcity Index—★**

**Jimi Hendrix** (1942-1970)—Hendrix and his band, the Jimi Hendrix Experience, are legendary among the rocker set. Many believe he is still unmatched in guitar skills although a host have tried to imitate him since his death. He signed for fans who met him, often adding "Stay Groovy" to his signature. If the band members signed a piece as well, it helps the value a little but not too much, as Hendrix alone is where the money's at. He currently sells as a signature for about $800, with signed photographs and album jackets at $2000 or more. A few documents in the same $2000-plus range have sold at auction as well.
**Scarcity Index—★★★★**

**The Isley Brothers** (Formed 1957)—First hitting the charts in 1957, the Isley Brothers are still at it today! Their biggest early hit was "Shout" followed by "Twist and Shout." Ten years later they hit number one with "It's Your Thing." The second generation tried to sing at the mikes, too—two younger brothers and a cousin—but to mixed success. They retired early in 1984. The original trio played on, however, until brother O'Kelly had a heart attack in 1986. Even then, brothers Ronald and Rudolph continued without him, releasing their last album in 1992. Expect to pay $100 plus for a signed photograph of the trio. (Jimi Hendrix was once one of many back up band members that played with them for a time.)
**Scarcity Index—★★★**

**Sam and Dave** (Formed 1960)—The original Blues Brothers, Sam Moore met Dave Prater in 1961 and soon was turning out hits like "Soul Man" and "Hold On, I'm Coming." They split up all too soon, however, to pursue solo careers, although neither had a big hit alone. In the late 1970s, The Blues Brothers, led by John Belushi and Dan Ackroyd, greatly revived interest in their music. Signed photographs of the pair are quite scarce with no current pricing available. However, Sam Moore-signed photographs can be had at around $60.
**Scarcity Index—Together★★★**

**The Yardbirds** (Formed 1963)—The Yardbirds was at various times made up of three of rock's greatest talents: Eric Clapton, Jeff Beck, and Jimmy Page. When the band released a pop hit instead of the blues-based rock he had signed on for, Clapton left the group. A few years later, Page left to form Led Zeppelin. Although not as successful in terms of big hits as others in the British invasion, the Yardbirds' blues-heavy metal style and henomenal guitar licks had a profound effect on the rock music landscape. The three on one signed photograph sells at $250 plus.
**Scarcity Index—★★★**

**In 1993, the Hall of Fame inducted the following eight artists:**

**Ruth Brown** (1928-   )—A Jazz and R&B vocalist that dominated the 1950s Black charts, Ruth Brown has sung for decades for her fans even having a hit Broadway show in the 1980s. She currently hosts public radio's weekly show "Blues Stage." She is a friendly signer and sometimes answers her fan mail. Signed photographs sell at $40, with signatures at $20.
**Scarcity Index—★**

**Cream** (Formed 1966)—Cream only performed together for two years, but in that time period had a profound effect on rock and heavy metal music. Eric Clapton formed the group with Jack Bruce and Ginger Baker. Fortunately for fans, an autograph dealer did a private signing of all three on an 8" x 10" photograph that can still be purchased at around $125.
**Scarcity Index—★**

**Credence Clearwater Revival** (Formed 1967)—CCR was the brain child of lead singer and songwriter John Fogarty. Dubbed "swamp rock" because of their Louisiana Bayou styling, they were more consistent hit makers than any other band, except the Beatles, in their time. One hit after another poured forth, including "Proud Mary," "Midnight Special," "Bad Moon Rising," "Suzie Q," "I Put a Spell on You," and more. The group had trouble accepting that John provided all of the writing and singing skills, and John's own brother, Tom, left the group in 1971. The bassist, Stu Cook, and drummer, Doug Clifford, never had solo hits, either. As you would imagine, only John has had solo success, most memorably with the hit "Put Me In Coach." When John's brother, Tom, died in 1990, John said there would never be a reunion tour. Vintage material signed by all is rare. No prices from the past year showed any signed photographs selling, but a vintage set of their four signatures on a piece of paper sold for $150. Signed photographs of John Fogarty alone sell for around $60.
**Scarcity Index—Entire group★★★★**

**The Doors** (Formed 1965)—The lead singer, Jim Morrison, pretty much was the Doors. Hits like "Light My Fire" will always be played on radio stations. Morrison's signature is uncommon, selling for $600 plus, when encountered. It was sometimes his habit to sign only "Jim," which is worth considerably less. The other three members of the group have signed many items for different autograph companies, with their collective signatures worth around $40. Most of the money, like most of the talent lies with Jim. A few endorsed checks of Morrison's have surfaced recently, selling at around $1100 each.
**Scarcity Index—Entire Group★★★ Jim alone ★★★★**

**Etta James** (1938-    )—From 1960 to 1970, James hit the charts an incredible twenty-four times, but fell into drinking and drug problems that stalled her career for years. Recently, a cleaned up Etta has started touring again, singing her old blues standards. She is usually a willing signer when encountered in clubs after gigs, with her signature worth approximately $20, and signed photographs at around $45.
**Scarcity Index—★★**

**Frankie Lymon and the Teenagers** (Formed 1955)—A legendary New York "doo wop" group consisting of Joe Negroni, Herman Santiago, Jimmy Merchant, Sherman Gates, and their thirteen-year-old lead singer, Frankie Lymon. Their first and biggest hit, "Why Do Fools Fall in Love," went number one, but bad blood split the group up after only two years, and Frankie died of a drug overdose at the age of 26 in 1968. The Jackson Five, Smokey Robinson, and others have all stated   that they patterned their early work after Frankie's groundbreaking style. Material is obviously rare on the group and Frankie, in particular. No recorded sells exist from last year to set a price on.
**Scarcity Index—★★★★★**

**Van Morrison** (1945-   )—One of the most critically-acclaimed singer/songwriters of pop music history. His over thirty years of hits like "Another Saturday Night," "Brown Eyed Girl," and "Wild Nights" are still covered by artists today. He still tours, and his lastest album was released in 1994. He is a bit reclusive and a tough signature to get, but he will on occasion sign. A signature is worth $40, with a signed photograph at around $75. **Scarcity Index**—★★★

**Sly and the Family Stone** (Formed 1966)—Sylvester Stone came into the psychedelic rock era in 1967 with the hit "Everyday People" spouting the band's multi-racial beliefs. They were, in fact, rock's first integrated band of black and white musicians. A string of hits followed like "Dance to the Music." Drug problems derailed the group's success, however, but years later, Kool and the Gang and KC and the Sunshine Band picked up in the same vein. A few vintage documents signed by the entire group sold in the $200 range recently. No signed photographs traded hands last year, but would be comparably priced. **Scarcity Index**—★★★

**In 1994, eight more members were inducted:**

**The Animals** (Formed 1960)—Lead singer Eric Burden formed the Animals with John Steel, Alan Price, and Hilton Valentine. Quickly shooting to the top of both British and American charts with the song "House of the Rising Sun," the Animals had arrived. A string of hits followed over the next two years, like "We've Gotta get Outta This Place," but different rifts began to develop within the group. Alan Price left in late 1965 and was replaced by Dave Rowberry. Then, in 1966, Steel left, replaced by Barry Jenkins. Chandler left next that same year and the constant band member changes kept the group from concentrating on hitmaking. Eventually, after many valiant efforts, Burden disbanded the Animals in 1971 and joined the group War, before embarking on a solo career. Vintage material would need to have Burden as a signer and any of the above mentioned combinations. No signed photograph sold in the past year to note price, but a vintage document signed by all has sold for $450.
**Scarcity Index—★★★★**

**The Band** (Formed late 1950s)—Four Canadians and one American—Robbie Robertson, Garth Hudson, Richard Manuel, Rick Danko, and Levon Helm—formed The Band to play back up for artist Ronnie Hawkins through eight of his chart hits, before moving on to being Bob Dylan's back-up band. Touring over the years with Dylan, they released eight of their own albums, which were greatly admired by peers. The Band never achieved huge commercial success, but continued to experiment and challenge current trends. Though Richard Manuel committed suicide in 1986, the Band still performs today with assorted new members. A signed photograph of the original group runs approximately $150.
**Scarcity Index—★★★**

**Duane Eddy** (1938-   )—Probably the most influential instrumentalist of the 1950s and 1960s rock era, he even helped popularize the electric guitar. He enjoyed fifteen Top 40 hits from 1958 to 1963. Most memorable of all are the songs "Peter Gunn Theme" and "Rebel Rouser." Although by the time of the British Invasion he was finished commercially, he still performs today. Signed photographs sell at around $60, with signatures at $30.

**Scarcity Index—★★★**

**The Grateful Dead** (Formed 1965)—The longest run commercially of any of the 1960s acid rock bands, the Grateful Dead played to sold out arenas full of "Deadheads" until late in 1995, when leader Jerry Garcia died of a heart attack. Through nearly thirty years, the band was constantly evolving, both in their music and in their lineup, with Phil Lesh, Bill Kreutzman, Bob Weir, and Garcia the constants.  Ron McKennan died in 1973, and keyboardist Keith Godchaux died in a 1979 car accident, shortly after he and wife, Donna, left the band. The next keyboardist, Brent Mydland, died in 1990 of a drug overdose. Vince Welnick, formerly of the Tubes, was added to replace Mydland, and Grammy-winner Bruce Hornsby played over 100 shows with the band, as well. All living members are fairly friendly signers when approached, but Garcia is now the key. Garcia alone on a signed photograph can bring $250, with the entire group on photographs selling at $550 plus. A few documents surfaced recently that brought $700 at auction.

**Scarcity Index—★★★**

**Elton John** (1947-  )—The partnership of writer Bernie Taupin with singer/composer Elton John has prospered for nearly 30 years and through dozens of well-known hits. After the tragic death of Princess Diana in 1997, John re-recorded his Marilyn Monroe tribute song "Candle in the Wind" in honor of the Princess, changing the lyrics to mirror her life. The single has sold over 40 million copies to date, making it the single biggest selling record in pop history. Now that John has a home he enjoys in Atlanta, Georgia, he is more available to sign and has done so at Tower Records and in person quite often. His signed photographs sell around $55, with signatures at $25.
**Scarcity Index—★★**

**John Lennon** (1940-1980)—Lennon was covered under our earlier Beatles entry and in the main part of the book. Please refer to those sections for information about him.

**Bob Marley** (1945-1980)—A RARE signature that commands $600-700 and upwards of $1500 plus on an album or photograph. The King of the Reggae sound was always a tough signer and, to compound problems, he died of cancer in 1980.
**Scarcity Index—★★★★★**

**Rod Stewart** ( 1945-  )—Starting as lead singer with the group "Faces" and hitting the charts with the song "Maggie May," Stewart eventually went solo with hit after hit for the next twenty five years. Married to actress/model Rachel Hunter, he is a fairly nice signer when encountered, with signed photographs selling for $60, and signatures at $25.
**Scarcity Index—★★**

**In 1995, the Hall of Fame inducted eight more artists, including:**

**Allman Brothers Band** (Formed 1969)—The southern rock of the 1970s had many influences and the vocal and guitar work of these two brothers was certainly one. Duane and Gregg Allman, along with Dickey Betts, Berry Oakley, and Butch Trucks made up the group. One hit followed another until Duane died in a motorcycle accident, followed by the death of Oakley in another motorcycle accident. Still, the remaining brother Gregg trudged on to have a hit with "Rambling Man" and cut several more albums before the group split up in 1975. Pieces signed by both brothers are scarce, selling at $100 for a pair of signatures, and $200 plus on a signed photograph. Gregg is still a friendly signer, with his signature selling at $20, and photographs at around $40.
**Scarcity Index—Entire group★★★★**

**Al Green** (1946-    )—The Reverend Al Green became a pastor of the Full Gospel Tabernacle Church in Memphis, Tennessee, turning his back on a musical career that spanned fifteen Top Ten records and thirteen more Top 40 hits. He is a willing signer to this day, with signed photographs selling at $45, and signatures at $20.
**Scarcity Index—★★**

**Janis Joplin** (1943-1970)—One of the most flamboyant of the overdose rockers, the "Pearl," as her fans nicknamed her, had a bawdy career on and off stage, with such southern rock classics as "Ball and Chain" and the Kris Kristofferson song, "Me and Bobby McGee." She was a friendly signer when encountered, often adding XXX (Kisses) marks after her name, but due to her overdose at such a young age at the height of her fame, the supply is almost always outstripped by demand. A signature sells at around $750, with signed photographs and albums selling for as much as $2000.

**Scarcity Index**—★★★★

**Led Zeppelin** (Formed 1968)—Jimmy Page (who had just left the group the Yardbirds), Robert Plant, John Paul Jones, and John Bonham formed what would become one of the first mega rock bands in the 1970s. They released an incredible eight Top Ten albums with hits like "Stairway to Heaven" and "Whole Lotta Love." Bonham died in 1980 and the band called it quits. Signed photographs of the original group sell for around $500 currently, about $150 less without Bonham.

**Scarcity Index**—★★★

**Martha and the Vandellas** (Formed 1963)—One of the first and best of the Motown female groups, Martha Reeves formed the group around her distinctive vocals for a series of hits that included "Heat Wave" and "Dancing in the Streets." They disbanded in 1969. In 1989, they reunited for the retro oldies circuit, where Reeves performs to this day with original Vandellas Rosalind Holmes and Annette Beard, all of whom are friendly signers, with signed photographs selling at around $75.

**Scarcity Index**—★★

**The Orioles** (Formed 1947)—A legendary pioneering group in rock who in the late 1940s and early 1950s caused the shift from pop harmonies to doo wop styled music. Their most memorable hit was probably "Crying in the Chapel." No prices exist currently, as there were no recorded sales of autographed items from the group last year.
Scarcity Index—★★★★★

**Neil Young** (1945-  )—Starting with Buffalo Springfield in 1966, Young next went solo when the band broke up in 1968. In 1969, he joined the band Crosby, Stills and Nash until their split up the following year, when he went solo again. Solo work and hit records like "Heart of Gold" followed. In 1989, over twenty years after his first hit, he had a new gold album and the respect of many new groups like Pearl Jam, who proclaimed him the Godfather of Grunge music. He is still releasing albums and touring, and although sometimes tough to get to, he will, on occasion, sign for fans, with a signature at around $35, and a signed photograph at around $60.
Scarcity Index—★★★

**Frank Zappa** (1940-1993)—One of rock and roll's most prolific artists, perhaps releasing more music than any other over the years. His sarcastic wit and ingenious style matched with expert guitar licks built him a large fan base. He was always a friendly signer signing "F.Zappa" when he did sign for fans. His signature is getting tougher to find, as he died of cancer in December of 1993. His signature is currently valued at about $100, with signed photographs and albums at $200. A few documents have sold in the same $200 range.
Scarcity Index—★★★

**In 1996, the Hall of Fame inducted the following seven acts into their prestigious ranks:**

**Gladys Knight and the Pips** (Formed 1952)—One of the most respected of soul singers, Gladys started singing as a child and was still a teen when she formed the group, along with her brother Merald and two cousins. Although signed to a small record label in 1961, it would be her 1966 move to Motown that would really launch her career, with hits like "I Heard it Through the Grapevine" and "If I Were Your Woman." She left Motown in the 1970s, but still had hits like the classic "Midnight Train to Georgia." The Pips retired shortly after, and she has been singing solo from then on, never hitting high on the charts again, but still selling out rooms wherever she plays. She has always been a gracious signer, with her signature selling for $25, and photographs at around $55. A few vintage documents signed by her and the Pips have sold in the $200 range. **Scarcity Index—★**

**Jefferson Airplane** (Formed 1965)—Jefferson Airplane was the hottest of the hippie, free love era 1960s bands. Their performance at Woodstock was legendary as was their outspoken lead singer Grace Slick, who formed the group along with Paul Kantner and Marty Balin. In 1974, they changed their name to Jefferson Starship and had a huge hit "Miracles." Grace Slick then left the group from 1976 to 1981, and Micky Thomson joined them in 1979. In 1984, Kantner left the group, and they added Donny Baldwin and Pete Sears to the lineup, and had their biggest selling number one hit, "We Built This City." In 1987, Sears left and they had another number one hit, but in 1988 when Slick left again, the remaining trio called it quits, and became studio musicians. The various members have always been willing signers. A signed album sells for around $200, with the original lineup on it.

**Scarcity Index**—★★

**Little Willie John** (1937-1968)—If you have never heard of John, do not feel bad. Great soul pioneers like Sam Cooke, Al Green, Clyde McPhatter, and B.B. King have all said that he is the most overlooked of the soul pioneers. His short career, which lasted from the early 1950s to mid 1960s, ended when he stabbed a man in a fight in 1964. He was sent to prison, where he died of pneumonia in 1968. The year he died, James Brown put out a tribute album in his honor, and huge acts like Fleetwood Mac and the Beatles have recorded his songs. He is very rare as a signature, and none traded hands last year for us to track prices on, but expect to pay a couple of hundred dollars for a signature.

**Scarcity Index**—★★★★★

**Pink Floyd** (Formed 1966)—From their humble beginnings in 1965 until the end, Pink Floyd never strayed from the experimental edge of rock music. Light shows, big theatrical concerts, and sound effects were a few other pioneering moves the band took. Band leader Syd Barrett, who named the group and wrote their first album, left the group due to drug problems, leaving Roger Waters as sole songwriter, and Dave Gilmour. The group hit big with their next LP called *Dark Side of the Moon*, which hit number one on the album charts and set records for riding those charts for over a year. In fact, the next several albums were all well received with *The Wall* also hitting the number one spot. Gilmour and Waters broke up the group in 1983, although Gilmour reformed it in 1987 with new members Nick Masani and Rick Wright. They continue to tour and release albums, but it is the original Waters and Gilmour that are needed and collected on signed photographs which are valued at $250-300.
**Scarcity Index—★★★**

**Pete Seegar** (1919-   )—Undoubtedly the greatest influence on folk/pop music, Seeger has scored folk hits since the 1930s. He has also written many hits for other bands, including "Turn, Turn, Turn" for the Byrds. In his late 70s, he still hustles from appearance to appearance and is a very gracious signer, with signatures selling at $15, and signed photographs at $30.
**Scarcity Index—★**

**The Shirelles** (Formed 1957)—One of the most successful girl groups of the 1960s, the Shirelles hit the Top Ten 6 times in only three years, with hits like "Soldier Boy" and "Will You Still Love Me Tomorrow?" Although they recorded into the 1970s, they never hit the Top 40 after 1963. The three women who met while in high school together have signed fan mail and are friendly signers in person. A signed photograph recently sold for $100.

Scarcity Index—★★★

*Love*
*Shirley Alston*
*Reeves*
*original leader of*
*The Shirelles*

**The Velvet Underground** (Formed 1966)—Pop artist Andy Warhol sponsored the Velvet Underground's emergence onto the pop scene and even added a German singer friend of his (Nico) to their group. Lou Reed wrote most of the songs and, with Johnny Cale, Sterling Morrison, and Maureen Tucker, the band was set to rock and roll. Problem was they wrote about what they knew—drug overdoses, transexuality, and other topics which kept them from much airplay. The inside joke in rock is that although the VU did not sell many albums, everyone who bought one formed a band. Mega group REM admits to the VUs influence on their music. Reed left after the first of four LPs were released and Cale after the second, but a majority of the members, including certainly Reed, is needed from a collecting standpoint. All of the members are alive and accessible and some have signed fan mail. A reunion tour in Europe by the original band members happened in 1993. A signed photograph sells for around $150.

Scarcity Index—★★★

# CLUB NAMES AND COLLECTING ORGANIZATIONS

Currently, there are two very fine clubs that you can belong to as a collector or a dealer. Both issue periodic magazines to their subscribers that, in themselves, are worth more than the dues. The oldest club in existence and the largest is the Universal Autograph Collectors Club (UACC) with thousands of members, and a fine magazine called the *Penn and Quill*, which is issued quarterly. The dues to join are only $22 per year and you may join or find out more about the organization by writing:

> **UACC**
> Chris Wilson/Secretary
> P.O. Box 6181
> Washington, DC  20044
> ★

The second organization is for the serious collector of letters of famous people, hence the name Manuscript Society. If you feel your collecting interests lie in that direction, they can be reached at:

> **The Manuscript Society**
> 350 N. Niagara Street
> Burbank, CA  91505-3648
> ★

Or you may join them by sending in $35 for a one year membership.  Members joining after July 1 may pay half the annual rate.

You will find dealers of autographs displaying both of these organization's logos in their advertising if they are members in good standing, which is important as a means of protecting you as a consumer. Both organizations will handle unresolved complaints, should any arise between yourself and a dealer, and even in extreme cases kick a dealer out of the organization for shady business practices. They also both put out top notch information to members via newsletters and magazines that will help you in your collecting.

The standard price guide to autographs in all fields, with over 50,000 autographs listed, has been published for years by collectors/historians George and Helen Sanders. *The Sanders Price Guide to Autographs* sells for $24.95 and is an indispensible reference guide to collectors. It also illustates over 1500 authentic autographs to compare yours with, as well as several interesting chapters on different collecting fields. You may order a copy by calling 1-888-689-7079.

# Major Dealers and Auction Houses

Listed here is by no means a listing of every reputable auction or autograph company in existence; however, we have endeavored to list the ones that have been around the longest (on average ten or more years) and that issue regular catalogs or auctions in all fields of autograph collecting. You should call or write these fine organizations for a copy of their latest catalogs, or if you have material you would like to consign or sell to them. Incidentally, no one in the following list asked to be included or paid for the right to be. Rest assured these are among the finest dealers in the field.

**Piece of the Past, Inc**
2240 Palm Beach Lakes Blvd. Suite 310
West Palm Beach, FL 33409
1-888689-7079

★

**Gallery of History**
3601 West Sahara Avenue
Las Vegas, NV 89102
1-800-425-5379

★

**University Archives**
600 Summer Street
Stamford, CT 06901
1-800-237-5692

★

**Profiles in History**
345 N. Maple Drive, Suite 202
Beverly Hills, CA 90210
310-859-7701

★

**Walter Burks Autographs**
PO Box 23097
Stanley, KS 66283
1-913-897-4674

★

**Max Rambod Autographs**
9903 Santa Monica Blvd., Suite 371
Beverly Hills, CA 90212
1-310-475-4535

★

**Cordelia and Tom Platt**
2805 E. Oakland Blvd
Ft. Lauderdale, FL 33306
1-954-564-2002

**Les Perline and Co.**
Two Gannett Drive, Suite 200
White Plains, NY 10604
1-800-567-2014

★

**Steven Raab Autographs**
Box 471
Ardmore, PA 19003
1-610-446-6193

★

**Robert Batchelder**
1 West Butler Avenue
Ambler, PA 19001
1-215-643-1430

★

# ABOUT THE AUTHOR

Kevin Martin has been a full-time dealer in autographs for 15 years, although he has collected since he was a child. His first autograph gallery opened eight years ago and his company, Piece of the Past, issues monthly catalogs to collectors and dealers, as well as conducting four auctions per year.

Martin has written articles on the subject of autographs for years, which have appeared in dozens of newspapers and magazines, including his long-running feature, "Fakes, Frauds and Forgeries" in *Autograph Collector* magazine.

He has served as a consultant for nearly every major auction house, and is the associate editor of *The Sanders Price Guide to Autographs*, which is a standard in the field. He also hosts "Showbiz Collectibles," the longest running national TV show on a home shopping channel, the Video Catalog Channel.